THE GLORY OF
ROSES

PHOTOGRAPHS BY CHRISTOPHER BAKER
TEXT BY ALLEN LACY

STEWART, TABORI & CHANG
NEW YORK

Captions by Allen Paterson

Floral arrangements by Robyn W. Fairclough with the assistance of Susan Ward;
interior locations courtesy of Ms. Lisa Krieger and Mrs. H. Serrell.

Hardcover edition published in 1990 and
paperback edition published in 1995 by
Stewart, Tabori & Chang, a division of U.S. Media Holdings, Inc.
575 Broadway, New York, New York 10012

Library of Congress Cataloging-in-Publication Data

Lacy, Allen, 1935–
The glory of roses / photographs by Christopher Baker ; text
by Allen Lacy.
p.   cm.
Includes bibliographical references.
ISBN 1-55670-155-1 (Hardcover)
ISBN 1-55670-448-8 (Paperback)
1. Roses.   2. Roses—Pictorial works.   3. Rose culture.
I. Baker, Christopher.   II. Title.
SB411.L28   1990
635.9′33372—dc20   90-34496
                                                                                       CIP

Distributed in the U.S. by Stewart, Tabori & Chang,
575 Broadway, New York, NY 10012.
Distributed in Canada by General Publishing Company Limited,
30 Lesmill Road, Don Mills, Ontario, Canada M3B 2T6.
Distributed in the U.K. by Hi Marketing,
38 Carver Road, London SE24 9LT, England.
Distributed in Europe by Onslow Books Limited,
Tyler's Court, 111A Wardour Street, London W1V 3TD, England.
Distributed in Australia and New Zealand by Peribo Pty Limited,
58 Beaumont Road, Mount Kuring-gai, NSW 2080, Australia.

Printed in Japan

1 3 5 7 9 8 6 4 2

Page 1: *Seen through a rain-washed window, these roses have a dreamy, painterly effect.* Page 2–3: *A glorious, extravagant bouquet of roses displays a harmonious array of color and form.* Page 4: *Magnificent roses such as these can be found throughout the historic gardens at Cranborne Manor, Dorset.* Page 5: *These blooms in a South Carolina garden are a rosarian's delight.* Page 7, top: *Large-flowered roses as well as miniatures can be successfully grown in containers;* bottom: *The beauty of this velvety rose from Field Farm, Kent, is further enhanced by soft morning light.* Page 8–9: *Against the crumbling wall of an Italian villa, a graceful climbing rose provides a spray of warm color.* Page 10: *Delicate in appearance, roses are strong, long-lived plants that provide beauty season after season.* Pages 14–15: *Wonderfully scented and easy to grow, Rosa rugosa flourishes in sandy soil bordering the coast of New England.*

CONTENTS

PREFACE AND ACKNOWLEDGMENTS

I LAY NO claim to being an expert on roses, as regards their care and cultivation. What fascinates me most about these plants is the love and affection they have called forth in human beings from ancient times to the present day—and for the foreseeable future. Roses are the universal flower. If there is anyone who knows the name of only one kind of flower, that one will surely be the rose. Sacheverell Sitwell put it perfectly in *Old Fashioned Flowers* (1935): "The rose has that preponderance, that popularity and practicality, that is possessed, in the world of music, by the pianoforte." Sitwell's point is apt, for the music written for the piano far exceeds that for any other instrument. Similarly, the literature about roses is vast. No other genus of plants has been written about so often and at such great length, from the sublime—Dante's vision of the Mystic Rose at the end of "Il Paradiso"—to the pedestrian—advice on pruning roses and protecting them from insects and disease.

I must confess that I grow only a few roses in my own garden. I am on much more intimate terms with the herbaceous perennials that are my first and longest love, with daylilies, peonies, hostas, and all the rest. What interested me in undertaking to write about roses was my first glimpse of Christopher Baker's photographs, which have an honesty rare in depictions of the rose. Baker shows withered roses as well as those in elegant bud or sumptuous full bloom, shows roses on tumbledown fences and in front of modest bungalows as well as those in famous and well-tended gardens in England and Europe. By the time I finished reading everything about roses I could lay hands on, there were stacks of books on roses piled high on my study floor, more on my library shelves, and still others in a heap by my bed table. Over a long winter of reading and writing, I have carried on a prolonged colloquy with rose lovers both quick and dead. This is the result.

I owe many debts. Chief of these is to my wife, Hella, who has been patient and mostly forgiving of the odd habits of someone who writes on plants and gardening. My agent, Helen Pratt, has unfailingly answered my phone calls, lending a willing ear and cheerful encouragement. Elisabeth Woodburn of Booknoll Farm in Hopewell, New Jersey, and Paulette Rickert of Capability's Books in Deer Park, Wisconsin, have provided invaluable bibliographical assistance and advice. There is not the space here to acknowledge every debt, but for the help they gave I must mention John Barstow, Sandra Bierbrauer, Thomas Christopher, John Elsley, Joanne Ferguson, Nancy Goodwin, Tessa Goldsmith, Lorraine Hartman, Steve Hutton, and Ann Lovejoy.

January 1990

THE
LOVE OF
ROSES

It is curious, when one comes to think of it, how large a space the rose idea occupies in the world. It has almost a monopoly of admiration. In love and literature, ancient and modern, it is a leading figure. A mysterious something in its nature—an inner fascination, a subtle witchery, a hidden charm which it has and other flowers have not—ensnares and holds the love of the world.

—CANDACE WHEELER, *Content in a Garden* (1902)

I

F THE SIGHT of roses, or their delicate fragrance, has been generally delightful and pleasing, there have also been those who could not endure them," wrote the American nurseryman Samuel B. Parsons in *The Rose: Its History, Poetry, Culture, and Classification* (1847). "Anne of Austria, wife of Louis XIII of France, although otherwise very fond of perfumes, had such an antipathy to the rose, that she could not bear the sight of one even in a painting. The Duke of Guise had a still stronger dislike, for he always made his escape at the sight of a rose. Dr. Ladelius mentions a man who was obliged to become a recluse, and dared not leave his house, during the season of roses; because, if he happened to imbibe their fragrance, he was immediately seized with a violent cold in his head."

Parsons carries his catalog of the haters of the rose no farther than these three people, and for good reason: from very ancient times right up to the present, roses have loomed larger in human affections than any other plant. Lilies are their only near rivals in the length of their association with human beings and with our gardens. Roses grew in the Egypt of the Pharaohs. They were cultivated in Bronze Age Crete; one of the

This informal spot in a California mixed garden belies the glamour of gardens devoted solely to the rose. PRECEDING PAGE: *As in all fashions, preferences in roses run their circle, from the full luxuriance of these blossoms to the delicacy of miniature teas and back again.* PAGE 16: *Deadheading, a winnowing of spent blossoms for future growth, ensures a long flowering season and leaves behind a flurry of color.*

THE GLORY OF ROSES

earliest depictions of the rose is in a fresco at Knossos dating over thirty-five hundred years ago. Coins minted in Rhodes at the beginning of the fifth century B.C. show a rose on one side, and Rhodes itself may mean "the place of roses," although not all scholars agree about this etymology.

Neither Plato nor Aristotle, as far as I know, mentioned roses, but Aristotle's disciple Theophrastus described several different species, but not in sufficient detail that modern botanists and horticulturists can identify them. The Greek poets Sappho and Anacreon sang the praises of the rose, Anacreon calling it the "Queen of Flowers." Homer, before them, spoke of Aurora, the goddess of dawn, as "rosy-fingered," and he described the shield of Achilles as adorned by roses. In Greek mythology the rose was associated with Aphrodite, in Roman mythology with Venus. The Roman naturalist Pliny the Elder gave many pages to roses in his

Generally considered a form of Rosa gallica, *Complicata has elegant single flowers that give no clue as to the origin of its name.*

THE GLORY OF ROSES

20

Natural History, written in the last quarter of the first century A.D. Virgil and Horace both wrote admiringly of roses, which their fellow citizens held high in esteem and affection. Christians early found symbolic links between the rose and both the Virgin Mary and Christ, and the rich symbolism accumulated ever greater and greater power in the Middle Ages and the early Renaissance.

No flower has figured more prominently than the rose in the history of art, from Botticelli to Georgia O'Keeffe. No flower, furthermore, has received such attention from poets. The rose is a central image in both Dante's *Divina Commedia* and the thirteenth-century *Romance of the Rose*. Shakespeare, Herrick, Campion, Blake, both the Brownings, Wordsworth, Yeats, Eliot—all wrote poems on roses, as did so many others that it would be easier to list poets who ignored the rose than those who paid it

As frail as a butterfly, this single Chinese rose holds the raindrops. OVERLEAF: *The informality of a climbing rose contrasts with boxwood topiary and pleached lindens, enriching the distinctly Italian countryside.*

THE GLORY OF ROSES

court. Eastern poets such as Omar Khayyám offered their praise as did such highly forgettable poets as Felicia Hemans and Louisa Ann Twamley, about whom I know only that they wrote in English in the nineteenth century and that they wrote, respectively, "A Song of the Rose" and "Flower Fantasies"—dreadful poems both, but sincere in their high regard for the queen of flowers.

Nor have garden writers neglected the rose, by any means. In my personal library I have fifty books, old and new, devoted exclusively to roses. If I decided to buy all the others I know about, I would have to triple my income to pay for them and also have to add a wing to our house to accommodate them. Besides Parsons in America, William Paul, Catherine Gore, Ellen Willmott, Gertrude Jekyll, and many other British writers of the past devoted entire books to roses.

Instant effect for Parisian gardens: hybrid teas, shrub rugosas, and even trained climbers can be bought off the street.

In our own time, the distinguished British rosarian Graham Stuart Thomas has written several books on roses, especially the old shrub roses of the nineteenth century, which he admires so much and has done so much to rescue from the oblivion of old, almost forgotten gardens. Thomas Christopher's *In Search of Lost Roses* explores a similar passion for old roses in the United States today. Roses were an ever-recurrent theme in the lapidary essays Vita Sackville-West wrote for the London *Observer* about her garden at Sissinghurst Castle in Kent. Henry Mitchell, in his collection of essays, *The Essential Earthman*, and in his weekly column for *The Washington Post*, praises roses every chance he gets. So does the young British writer Stephen Lacey in his book, *The Startling Jungle: Colour and Scent in the Romantic Garden*. In writing on roses, I am but one of what the preachers I heard as a boy used to call "the great crowd of witnesses."

Outside Zurich, a schrebergarten *combines flowers and vegetables true to ancient country tradition.*

Roses are virtually worshipped. They have been for ages, and those who love them constitute a widespread and populous communion of saints. The Spanish philosopher Miguel de Unamuno once wrote that grave trouble awaited anyone who attempted to give reasons for loving anything or anyone. He was perhaps echoing Blaise Pascal: "The heart has its reasons which reason does not know." Still, it is easy to understand the love of roses, which springs out of delight in their diversity of forms and colors, their often powerful fragrance, and the luxurious feeling they can give in June to a garden where they are planted in generous profusion. Here I defer to the Anglican clergyman S. Reynolds Hole, who was dean of Rochester Cathedral from 1887 until his death in 1904, at the age of eighty-four. *A Book about Roses*, which he published in 1869, was one of the first books to earn the name of bestseller, and went through twenty editions during his lifetime. Hole, who once compared visiting a garden of

The nature of classicism is preserved by attention to detail as seen in the remarkable simplicity and grandeur of these arranged roses.

beautiful roses to hearing the "Hallelujah Chorus" for the first time, sung by a choir of a thousand voices, wrote this loving description of the varied charms of such a garden.

Enter, then, the Rose-garden when the first sunshine sparkles in the dew, and enjoy with thankful happiness one of the loveliest scenes of earth. What a diversity, and yet what a harmony of colour! There are White Roses, Striped Roses, Blush Roses, Pink Roses, Rose Roses, Carmine Roses, Crimson Roses, Scarlet Roses, Vermilion Roses, Maroon Roses, Purple Roses, Roses almost Black, and Roses of a glowing Gold. What a diversity, and yet what a harmony, of outline! Dwarf Roses and Climbing Roses, Roses closely carpeting the ground, Roses that droop in snowy foam like fountains, and Roses that stretch out their branches upward as if they would kiss the sun; Roses in shape no bigger than an agate-stone on the fore-finger of an alderman, and Roses five inches

Catmint, mock orange, and lady's mantle join thawing rosebuds awaiting re-arrangement as an early summer posy.

THE GLORY OF ROSES

across; Roses in clusters, and Roses blooming singly; Roses in bud, in their glory, decline, and fall. And yet these glowing tints not only combine, but educe and enhance each the other's beauty. All these variations of individual form and general outline blend with a mutual grace. And over all this perfect unity, what a freshness, fragrance, purity, splendour! They blush, they gleam amid their glossy leaves, and never . . . hath eye seen fairer sight.

If there is danger in asking about the reasons for love, there is a worse pitfall still in asking what love is good for. Love is, I think, its own value. If ever a man were smitten by love for anything, Dean Hole was smitten by the love of roses. In almost a conversion experience in 1844, he suddenly abandoned his former passion for foxhunting in order to grow his favorite flower. And he preached the Gospel of Roses as well as the Gospel of Christ. In 1856, feeling that it was wrong that the dianthus and the

ABOVE: *At Cranborne Manor, Dorset, a wichuraiana climber entices the garden stroller to the balustrade on one level, only to spill over onto the wall of the white garden below.* OPPOSITE: *One of a series of rose-covered arches that frame the beautiful vistas at Jenkyn Place, Hampshire.*

THE GLORY OF ROSES

primrose, but not the rose, should have flower shows devoted to them every year, he goaded his fellow rose-lovers to organize. Two years later, England's first National Rose Show was held under his direction. The show, a great success, became an annual event, each year attracting more exhibitors and more visitors.

Hole, however, was a good Victorian as well as a rose-lover, and he saw the rose as an instrument of the moral improvement of humankind, not just of aesthetic and sensual pleasure. In *A Book about Roses* he reports with huge satisfaction that when he asked another rose-lover, described as one of "the labouring poor," how he managed to afford new and expensive varieties of roses, the answer came back: "By keeping away from the beershops!" Hole saw in the love of gardening in general and of roses in particular an agency for increasing human happiness and good will

ABOVE: *A luster jug, a lace curtain, and old roses to match.* OPPOSITE: *A thatched cottage in Hampshire, England, becomes a traditional bower of climbing roses.* OVERLEAF: *The simplest of rustic arches supports a rambler rose on a Kentish cottage.*

among men. "Get a man out of the dram and beer shops into the fresh pure air," he wrote, "interest him in the marvellous works of his God, instead of in the deformities of vice, give him an occupation which will add to his health and the comforts of his family, instead of destroying both, then build Revealed upon Natural Religion, and hope to see him a Christian." His words did not fall on deaf ears; one reviewer of the first edition of his book described it as a road "to the inner heart of the lower classes—the key to tastes dearer to them than beer-swilling."

I do not know whether there is any merit to the Victorian notion that just as our first parents fell in a Garden, there may be moral or spiritual redemption in gardening. But I do know this about roses: they are for many people the objects of deep and surpassing love and, as such, ends in themselves. But they are also the means of expressing friendship, feeling of cordiality, sympathy, and love for other people. To give someone

ABOVE: *Modern roses adorn ancient foundations in the Forum in Rome.* OPPO-SITE: *Delicate Daisy Hill is among the many varieties of roses represented at Mot-tisfont Abbey, Hampshire.* OVERLEAF: *Irises, peonies, dame's rocket, and roses still inspire artists in Monet's garden.*

THE GLORY OF ROSES

flowers, whether it be a bouquet picked in your own garden or something from a florist shop, is to express kind regard for another human being, be it friend or lover, parent or child, or anyone else you wish to honor. The flowers will fade and wither in a short time, but the affections they expressed linger on and on—even if they too one day will be forgotten with time's passage.

Not long ago, while sorting through one of my mother's scrapbooks after Alzheimer's disease had stolen from her the last shred of memory and then of consciousness, I found a pressed rose—its browned petals still touched with red—with a card and a date. "I love you, Jetta," it said, and the date was 1924. She was sixteen then. I don't know who sent her the rose. It could have been my father, but I suspect not. That faded rose tells me now, many years after it blossomed, that someone loved my mother when she was only sixteen. Something important is told to me by a rose.

A BOVE: *Single roses turn into semi-double flowers when their stamens become petaloid; this type of sport prompted development into fully double flowers.* OPPO-SITE: *Fresh cut roses add wealth to a momentary resting place in a hallway.*

THE GLORY OF ROSES

ROSES IN GARDENS

He who would have beautiful Roses in his garden must have beautiful Roses in his heart. He must love them well and always. To win, he must woo, as Jacob wooed Laban's daughter, though drought and frost consume. He must have not only the glowing admiration, the enthusiasm, and the passion, but the tenderness, the thoughtfulness, the reverence, the watchfulness of love.

—S. REYNOLDS HOLE, *A Book about Roses* (11th ed., 1901)

A GARDEN WITHOUT roses is almost inconceivable. I say this as someone who grows only a few favorite roses, none of which would much impress rose connoisseurs. I have great affection for Betty Prior, which bears deep pink, single flowers unstintingly from late May until the first frost. Even afterwards it still may bloom sparsely, some years as late as Christmas, when any flower in the garden is welcome. I also admire my one plant of Climbing Peace, in a far corner of the garden where it scrambles up into a blue Atlas cedar by a sidewalk. It has shiny, deep green, almost-leathery foliage, and its color, peachy pink suffused with apricot yellow, satisfies the soul. Its buds are magnificently elegant and pointed, and they open into huge, sumptuous, and long-lasting flowers that command attention when brought inside for arrangements. Even just one flower in a bud vase is cheering. This Climbing Peace is so robust and healthy that in the seventeen years since I planted it I have never had to spray it with the pesticides that I oppose on principle but occasionally resort to in covert practice. The plant is just beyond reach of my water hoses and sprinklers, but it has not flagged even in years of bad drought. Roses have the reputation, sometimes deserved,

Against the light, the rich color of full pink roses epitomizes the freshness of a late June morning. PRECEDING PAGE: *Antique statuary and modern roses combine to provide a romantic garden setting at La Pietra, near Florence.* PAGE 40: *A simple rose arch divides the flower garden from the tool shed, adding color and beauty to both.*

THE GLORY OF ROSES

43

of being finicky and temperamental, but this one is a real toughie and I tip my hat to its grit and pluck. Its one real flaw is a complete lack of fragrance. (One nursery catalog in my collection puts the matter euphemistically, claiming for it "a gentle fragrance.")

Climbing Peace originated in the late 1940s as a mutation of Peace, the rose that may fairly be described as the best-known rose since 1945 and perhaps of the century. Peace was bred in the 1930s by the French hybridizer Francis Meilland. Cuttings were shipped to Conard-Pyle, a leading American rose nursery, on the last airplane to leave Paris as World War II began. It was given its American and English name—Peace—on the day Berlin fell to the Allies. As of 1974, one hundred thousand plants had been sold in Europe and America, but nobody seems to have kept count since.

ABOVE: *At Field Farm in Kent, the delicate pink rose is set off by rich purple, true red, and deep green in a marvelous combination of nature and design.* OPPO-SITE: *In this wonderfully complete garden scene, where clematis and roses share a support above foxgloves, irises, and meadow rue, not an inch of space is wasted.* OVERLEAF: *Bush roses add early summer color to this stately but otherwise monochromatic classical garden of cypresses, pines, and boxwood.*

THE GLORY OF ROSES

Other roses that I grow and value include several hybrids of the Oriental species *Rosa rugosa*. These roses are unusually well suited for the sandy soil of my garden at the New Jersey Shore, since their native habitat in China, Japan, and Korea is on coastal plains where they grow almost to the water's edge. The species has naturalized in parts of the United States to grow wild, covering acres of dunes on Cape Cod and Nantucket. In my garden I have Blanc Double de Coubert, which produces crop after crop of faintly scented, white double flowers that look much like gardenias, and my other treasured rugosa hybrids: Fru Dagmar Hastrup, with single blossoms of light, clear pink, and Sarah Van Fleet, with double flowers of a deeper shade of pink.

A few other roses round out what I dare not speak of as a "collection," at least not within the hearing of rosarians or true specialists. Four more

In early summer at Giverny, the ponds where Monet painted his famous Nymphéas *series are surrounded by roses and irises.*

THE GLORY OF ROSES

are also climbers, grown on a wooden rail fence where they don't take up a great deal of room. Dortmund has a fine single flower, boasting a Harvard crimson with a snowy blotch at the center. New Dawn is blush pink, with glossy green leaves; it blooms heavily in June, then intermittently the rest of the summer, with a fairly heavy crop of flowers in September. Gloire de Dijon is an orangish pink, Mme Alfred Carrière a creamy white. These latter two were hybridized in France in the middle of the nineteenth century and have one trait in common, powerful fragrance.

I am also fond of my Grüss an Aachen, an old rose bred early in the twentieth century by a German with the wonderfully appropriate surname Geduldig, which means "patient" in German. This low and shrubby plant, with very full flowers that open deep pink and then fade towards cream, is in bloom almost constantly from June to October. And,

Mottisfont Abbey, Hampshire, now holds the definitive collection of heritage roses brought together by the distinguished rosarian, Graham Stuart Thomas.

THE GLORY OF ROSES

Exceptional color combinations and balance of form distinguish Monet's garden at Giverny.

THE GLORY OF ROSES

for sentiment's sake, I have Cécile Brünner, the old-fashioned sweetheart rose that my grandmothers raised for its tiny, almost-perfect buds and its abundance of very small, flesh pink flowers.

One peculiarity of the rose, above every other flower, is that just one bush, carelessly planted and then left to its own devices in an unpromising location—say, clambering over a wire fence partially concealing a junk-yard, or in front of an ugly house painted a nasty shade of turquoise with a cigarette strewn sidewalk by the street—can suggest the possibilities of a garden, can be an incipient garden. That one rosebush may remain alone, the product of someone's one and only nod toward beauty—a stillborn impulse. But it may also spur the person who planted it toward ampler and more fulfilling ambitions in garden making. I don't know how many dedicated gardeners got their start by planting a rose, without larger horticultural intentions at the time, but the number must be large.

I have some strong opinions—healthy prejudices—about what gardens should be. In the gardens I most admire and in the garden I have tried to make of my own desire and design, roses are a part, a necessary part, but certainly not the entire ingredient. A garden ought to be a peaceable kingdom, where lions and lambs lie down together. Roses should live with violets and lady's mantle at their feet, and they should grow alongside daylilies and bee balm and gaura and other perennials. They should not be kept separate and apart, but should be allowed to mingle with nandinas and bayberries and mahonias and other shrubs, near sourwoods and purple-leafed plums and other small trees. When roses first bloom in June, the creamy white bells on the tall spires of yuccas should be in flower close to hand, especially for the enjoyment of the evening mingling of perfumes. I believe firmly in the mixed garden, in all-embracing horticultural catholicity.

I am not alone in this belief and preference. In fact, I am in the excellent, if sometimes persnickety, company of the great British hor-

OPPOSITE, ABOVE: *Striped roses have ever been popular and Rosa Mundi, said to celebrate Fair Rosamund, King Henry II's mistress, is one of the most acclaimed.* BELOW: *While American Pillar is one of the most robust of all rambler roses, it requires hard pruning and careful tying in for its success.*

---

ticulturist William Robinson. In all fifteen successive revised editions of his influential book *The English Flower Garden* published between 1883 and 1933, Robinson expressed some strong opinions about roses. They should be grown from cuttings so that they would produce their own root systems, rather than by being grafted or budded onto an understock of some other rose. Grafting was (and still is) a favored method of propagating roses by nurserymen because it produces many plants in short order. But Robinson was sure it ultimately resulted in weak plants that were subject to disease. He abhorred in particular the kind of grafting that produced tree roses or standards: "roses stuck and mostly starving on the tops of sticks," he wrote. Robinson also thought that mulching roses with a mixture of straw and "excreta from the farm" was "anything but a sanitary or even necessary thing to do," preferring instead to put pansies, violets,

Most roses are formidably armed: shrub roses with straight spines and climbers with hooked prickles, which enable them to scramble up and through their support.

and thymes beneath his roses. He was of the mind that the rose gardens he saw in Paris were "sickly."

But the strongest of his opinions was that the practice, common in his day, of growing roses in a separate garden, apart from other plants, was a "stupid notion" that impoverished both roses and other plants. "There is great loss to the flower garden from the usual way of growing the Rose as a thing apart, and its absence at present from many flower gardens. It is surprising to see how poor and hard many places are to which the beauty of the Rose might add delight, and the only compensation for all this blank is what is called the rosery, which in large places is often an ugly thing with plants that usually only blossom for a few weeks in summer."

Despite Robinson's advice and his influence, there are many gardens still where roses rule entirely. Many of these are private gardens, and they

Full, rounded flowers of hybrid perpetuals such as these were the ideal of nineteenth-century rose gardens. OVERLEAF: *Deadheading, cutting off blossoms past their bloom, will ensure further breathtaking displays of this vivid grandiflora rose now in its first summer flush.*

THE GLORY OF ROSES

are the result of sectarian impulses. By sectarian impulses I mean, in the world of gardening, a fairly common phenomenon in which people's affections are drawn to one genus of flowering plant and one genus only. They grow this genus to the exclusion of everything else, or if they grow anything else, they call it a "companion plant." They become collectors, trying to have as many different species and cultivars within a single genus as possible, no matter what the size of their gardens. They join societies of like-minded souls who share their singular passion and who can talk with them about rhododendrons, about hostas, about irises, without boredom on either side. They are the fern folks, the actinidia enthusiasts, the daylily devotees. But I respect horticultural passion wherever it occurs and in whatever form it takes, and I confess gladly that my own life as a gardener began when I was totally smitten by daylilies to the exclusion of almost every other plant—an infatuation not of short

In Parc Floral d'Apremont, an extravagant pergola of roses and both white and purple wisteria provides a parade of blossom.

duration. We catholic gardeners owe much to the sectarians; their close observation of many plants in a single genus eventually teaches us all which are the really worthy hostas, the daylilies we ought to have, and so on.

The private garden of someone whose mind is set on roses and roses alone most commonly is composed of strips of mown lawn separating long, rectangular beds just wide enough to accommodate lines of roses planted two abreast. The lawn is neatly clipped at the edges of the beds. Nothing is planted beneath the roses, but the soil is generally mulched, not with the straw and "excreta" that so offended William Robinson, but with tidier material such as buckwheat hulls, shredded bark, or cocoa hulls. The roses, almost without exception, will be modern hybrid teas, for several reasons. This is the class of rose we commonly see in florist shops, whose

Amid the beautiful blooms lurk telltale dark areas on leaves which may be the symptoms of the disfiguring and debilitating black spot disease.

buds are long and pointed and whose flowers are full and many petaled, but not so full that they seem blowsy. In the public mind this class of rose has come to signify "the" rose, the flower's perfect form and embodiment. Hybrid teas, furthermore, if properly tended keep blooming right through the summer into the fall. Selective breeding has given them a range of colors unmatched in other roses, including hot and tropical-looking oranges.

The no-nonsense design of these rose gardens is as plain and simple as anything ever dreamed up by Frank Lloyd Wright or at the Bauhaus. Function dictates form. The beds are narrow and they are separated by strips of grass so that the gardener has easy access to each rose to give it the

ABOVE: *Roses create a balance between the shapes of art and architecture at this Italian villa.* OPPOSITE: *In the rose garden at Bagatelle, some seven thousand roses are displayed in almost seven hundred different forms.* OVERLEAF: *Andrew Marvell's repose of "green thoughts in a green shade" is here shot through with a burst of red roses.*

care that it requires. And in a collection of hybrid tea roses, care *is* required. Anyone who has ever grown these roses successfully or watched neighbors who do so knows that these plants call for a lot of work—deadheading to remove spent blossoms, irrigating, fertilizing, spraying, pruning, and many other tasks.

Probably some people who start gardens of hybrid tea roses would drop the venture right away if they knew what work it would involve, what absorption it would require. It is equally true that others would say, "Well, I didn't know that, but I love the things anyway, so I'll just keep on." Here are some of the finer mysteries of human life: we are not always prudent, selfish, calculating, and intent on the bottom line that we sometimes take as the ultimate value. Even in someone obsessed by the entrepreneurial spirit, there may be the soul of an amateur, in the original and the best sense of the word. Caring for roses is often a purely personal source of satisfaction, a communion with part of the natural order. But sharing is sometimes part of the rose lover's life as well, when cut roses are given to friends for their enjoyment and delight.

For home gardeners who devote themselves solely to the rose, however, their devotion may become a matter of competition, a pursuit whose greatest satisfaction comes when they win a blue ribbon at a rose show. The sure sign of the intention to exhibit cut roses and vie with other growers for prizes is the protection given to especially promising stems. Among the plants in the long beds, strange things sprout: wooden stakes supporting metal cones reminiscent of the funnel atop the Tin Woodman's head in *The Wizard of Oz*. The cones protect the developing buds from scorching sunlight or from rain that might blemish the petals. Further protection may be given, just before the stems are cut for transport to a rose show, by a wrapping of cellophane.

To refer once again to William Robinson, he was quite crusty about rose shows and their effect. He expressed dismay that "the practice and

A white picket fence, shingles, and American Pillar roses form a classic combination dating from the early years of this century.

THE GLORY OF ROSES

*Wisteria and climbing roses begin to
reclothe this courtyard pergola near
Tours, France.*

views of the Rose exhibitors" had "most unfortunately ruled the practice of gardeners," who were thereby led to "take the prize-taker as a guide." Robinson's point was that the roses best suited for the show table were seldom the best roses for the mixed style of garden that he favored and that suitable roses for gardens were overlooked as a result of competitions. As someone who has never entered a rose or any other flower in a show and who intends to end his days that way, I understand Robinson's point. I do not subscribe to it, however, again because I believe that horticultural passions, including those that I don't share, call for respect.

The desire to win shows itself in many ways, some of which, such as breeding racehorses, are open only to a very privileged few. Roses, however, are a remarkably democratic and accessible flower and competition for recognition as the one who has grown the best-of-show is open to all. Roses are relatively inexpensive plants; no greenhouse is needed to raise them, as is necessary with orchids, for example. And because roses

Roses duplicate with color and whimsy the sturdy usefulness of fences at this French communal garden.

are vegetatively propagated, each and every plant of such hybrid teas as Tropicana or Royal Velvet is genetically identical, whether it grows in the garden of a great estate or in a small garden behind a modest house. If one individual blossom exceeds all the rest on the show table, the difference lies entirely in the nurture it has received, in the loving care that has been lavished on it.

But there are other gardens devoted entirely to roses which do not have as their intention the production of hybrid tea roses for the show table. They exist to celebrate the rose in all its forms, especially in early summer when almost all roses are blooming at once in lavish profusion. These are the great rose gardens of the world and are usually public or municipal gardens: in Rapperswil, Switzerland, in Zweibrücken, West Germany, in Portland, Oregon, in St. Albans, England to list only a few.

Perhaps chief among them is La Roseraie de l'Hay-les-Roses, just

The heavy-scented rambler Albertine welcomes the gardener to this garden plot in Tours, France.

THE GLORY OF ROSES

south of Paris. Occupying more than twenty-seven acres, with five acres devoted exclusively to roses, including hybrid teas, this garden is somewhat paradoxical in its effect because of the way it demonstrates the limitations of hybrid teas in contrast to other kinds of roses. The hybrid teas are fundamentally flower factories, bred to produce flowers over a long season of bloom that are good for cutting and that come in a wide range of colors. Except for a few climbers, their bushes grow only three feet tall or slightly taller and are kept squat, earthbound, and uninteresting in form by the annual regimen of pruning.

At the Roseraie de l'Hay, however, a variety of exuberant roses feast the eye. They grow on pillars, clamber up trellises and over arbors and pergolas. They cover arches in series along pathways to form tunnels where one may walk unscathed by thorns through sweet roses. The great climbers and the ramblers aspire to the heavens and then cascade downward in tumultuous bloom—especially two exuberant roses: Paul's Himalayan Musk Rambler, which bears graceful clusters of pale pink flowers on stems that can exceed thirty feet and Kiftsgate, a white rose which grows even taller. Both of these ramblers are well suited to grow up trees.

The large shrub roses expand outward, taking full possession of the space they occupy. They become notable presences in the garden in a way that makes hybrid teas look like muffins in comparison.

The lessons learned here, in a garden all of roses, may be applied to mixed gardens. Many of the roses other than the hybrid teas can soften the lines of walls. Roses marry well with architecture, giving flesh to what the British call the bones of the garden. Roses give a sense of almost-boundless profusion. The pillar roses in particular unite heaven and earth, for one looks up through their great masses of flowers to the sky above. Roses can be combined with other plants, interwoven through them. They are particularly fetching with clematis vines intermingling. The flowers of many of the clematises look themselves much like single roses, but they add the near-blues and the rich purples missing in the palette of the rose.

Carefully pruned and the young shoots successively tied in, the rose on the verge of springtime foliage still presents its own intricate beauty.

THE GLORY OF ROSES

THE
NAMES OF
ROSES

*The sorts of Roses are very numerous, and botanists find it very difficult to de-
termine with accuracy which are species and which are varieties, as well as
which are varieties of the respective species, on which account Linneaus, and
some other eminent authors, are inclined to think that there is only one real
species of Rose, which is* Rosa canina *or Dog Rose of the Hedges. . . .*

—THOMAS MAWE AND JOHN ABERCROMBIE
Universal Gardener and Botanist (1778)

THE WORLD OF roses is, at first ap-
proach, a world of the names of roses, and the names are bewildering in
their number.

It was not always thus. For several millennia in western Europe and
in the Middle East, roses were few in number and few—and very
indefinite—in name. In his *Natural History* the Roman naturalist Pliny the
Elder singled out fewer than twenty kinds of roses, each identified by the
name of a place where it grew—the rose of Praeneste, the rose of Cyrene,
the rose of Pangaeus, and the like.

Many centuries later the great English herbalist John Gerard com-
mented in his massive tome *The Herball, or General History of Plants* (1633
ed.) that "there are many kinds of Roses differing either in the bignesse of
the floures, or the plant it selfe, roughnesse or smoothnesse, or in the
multitude of the flowers, or in the fewnesse, or else in colour and smell: for
divers of them are high and tall, others short and low; some have five
leaves, others very many. . . . Moreover, some be red, others white, and
most of them or all, sweetly smelling, especially those of the garden." But

The allure of long-stemmed greenhouse roses captures the city sidewalk market.
PRECEDING PAGE: *The leaves of rose species and their primary hybrids
typically have seven leaflets—modern bush roses have five—a token of
nature's simplicity amid the rose's grandeur.* PAGE 72: *Introduced
in 1879, the famous hybrid perpetual Mme Alfred Carrière
produces fragrant flowers over a long period of time.*

THE GLORY OF ROSES

75

Gerard's discussion of roses takes up only twelve pages out of 1,630, and he lists but eighteen kinds, beginning with *Rosa alba*, the white rose. Few of the names he gives have any scientific standing as species names, for he wrote before the Swedish botanist Linnaeus gave the natural world of plants and animals greater fixity and order by developing a system of binomial nomenclature of genus and species. Until the end of the eighteenth century, European botanists and gardeners had a comparatively modest number of species to reckon with—perhaps some thirty in all native to northern Europe and the Mediterranean Basin.

Nor were all these species true species in the botanical sense of plants that share distinctive characteristics and come true from seed when one plant in a given species is crossed with another in that same species. Species evolve or come into being by natural selection, essentially by adaptation to the conditions of a natural habitat. Gardens, however, are

These heavy sprays of roses, their further flowering encouraged by deadheading as the petals fade, command a matronly respect.

artificial, not natural, habitats. Within them, plants change their traits in response to what gardeners do, either inadvertently or deliberately. For instance, dandelions—pretty but pesty spring weeds—under natural conditions most commonly produce flower stems that are from eight to fourteen inches tall, depending on the fertility and moisture of the soil. But there is also a greater variation in height, since there are also recessive genes for dwarfism which when paired produce dandelions that bloom on short stems, only an inch or two above the earth. If a lawn is mowed regularly and kept cropped, dandelions carrying the dominant gene for tall stems will not produce seed, but the genetic dwarfs will. The result is that in due course gardeners will still curse the dandelions that mar their lawns, but the dandelions they will curse will be short ones that have beautifully adapted to survive in a habitat where sharp blades of steel regularly and frequently shear the turf.

Gallica shrub roses surround this protected sitting area in a North Carolina garden with their beauty and heavy perfume.

The evolution of roses in gardens takes place in an altogether different way, in response to the will, the taste, and the pleasure of gardeners. Like any given species of plant, the several natural species of roses contain variations within each type. There may be significant mutations: a rose with white flowers may produce one stem with red or pink ones; or there may be a virtually thornless stem on a bush that is otherwise heavily armed; a fairly low shrub may produce a long cane; a single rose may mutate and begin bearing double flowers. Some of these changes may be passed on to offspring when seeds are produced and planted. Some may be passed on when the plant is propagated vegetatively by taking cuttings and rooting them.

Mutations are particularly important as one means of new roses coming into being. Part of the explanation lies in the fact that since roses are grown in such great numbers, the chance of detecting a mutation increases. Part also lies in the inherent tendency of certain roses to mutate more than others. The cultivar Mme Edouard Herriot, which was introduced in 1913, by 1933 had produced nineteen different mutations that were thought worthy of naming and introducing. Common sense suggests that there may have been many others that were not so worthy. Roses also change when hybridization occurs naturally, as when insect-borne pollen from a flower in one species reaches the stigma of a flower in another, producing seeds of mixed ancestry. We gardeners are observant creatures, and we are covetous of diversity and novelty, seizing on them when they appear and preserving them for the future.

It is a general rule of horticulture that the longer the history of an ornamental plant in gardens, the greater the variation it will have. Roses go back into deep antiquity, and those that have been grown in the Middle East and in Europe for many centuries—even millennia—are far from being recognized as simple species. This point is true even though a rose

The freshness of an early summer shower rests on this Albertine, a wichuraiana rambler introduced in 1921.

THE GLORY OF ROSES

THE GLORY OF ROSES

may have a seemingly straightforward scientific name. Three examples of European roses will suffice.

Linnaeus named one rose commonly grown in Europe *Rosa gallica*—the French or Gallic rose. He was mistaken about its origins in France, since its original habitat was far more likely to have been in eastern Europe or Asia Minor. Furthermore, long before Linnaeus this species had evolved into several distinct forms in gardens, differing in degree of fragrance, plant habit, and the color and number of petals. As far as the so-called damask rose, sometimes listed as *Rosa damascena*, I defer to those experts who insist that there are two forms (with many variations in each form). The summer damask and the autumn damask are both now thought to be hybrids, not species. The summer damask is *Rosa* × *damascena*, probably a hybrid between *Rosa gallica* and *Rosa phoenica*; the autumn damask is probably a cross between *Rosa gallica* and *Rosa moschata*. The third rose, the cabbage rose or *Rosa centifolia*, so deeply loved by

ABOVE: *While selection and breeding has created roses with dozens of petals, all truly wild roses have just five.* OPPOSITE: *A bower of roses, a book, and sunlight provide the perfect retreat.* OVERLEAF: *An ancient brick wall at Penshurst Place, Kent, uses roses to hide the cracks of ages.*

THE GLORY OF ROSES

81

seventeenth- and eighteenth-century Dutch painters, is now thought to have gallica ancestry.

This all sounds very complicated, but it is very simple in comparison with what happened to the rose in Europe and America beginning in the late eighteenth and early nineteenth centuries when "the four stud roses," as they later came to be known, arrived in England from China. Imported by representatives of the East India Company, these were garden plants, bought in Chinese nurseries, not species collected in the wild. The first of these, introduced in 1792, was Slater's Crimson China, named for Gilbert Slater, a company official. It was probably a variant or selected form of *Rosa chinensis*; the other three were probably hybrids between *Rosa chinensis* and *Rosa gigantea*, both native to China. The second of the four was Parsons' Pink China, named for one of the first rose enthusiasts to grow it in England, sometime before 1795. The third, Hume's Blush Tea-Scented China, made its appearance in 1809, bringing with it one of the most

This glimpse of a traditional hybrid tea at Sissinghurst conjures up the passion attached to the rose by its devotees, including Vita Sackville-West.

delicious scents of the entire genus *Rosa*. And the last of this quartet of studs was Parks' Yellow Tea-Scented China, collected by the Royal Horticultural Society in 1824. These Chinese imports when crossed among themselves and with the leading European garden roses—the several forms of damasks and gallicas—revolutionized the world of roses by introducing genes for repeated bloom, saturated color including intense pinks and yellows, and attractive foliage.

The early nineteenth century saw a virtual explosion of roses. The period was one of enormous European interest in new plants, both exotic species collected by merchants, diplomats, and professional plant explorers in Asia and other parts of the world with a rich flora to offer, and new cultivated varieties brought into existence by human hybridization—a recent addition to the accidental hybridization that had always been possible in a garden.

Darwin did not announce until 1859 his theory of evolution, with its

Saint Elizabeth defied a ban on charity, delivering loaves of bread to the poor; upon discovery she claimed she merely carried roses in her apron and lo and behold, roses they were. OVERLEAF: *Massed climbers and old-fashioned roses with catmint flourish in a Kentish garden.*

corollary that far from animal and plant species being static and fixed, new species of living things came into being and old ones passed into extinction. The Austrian monk Gregor Mendel had not yet begun crossing peas to figure out the laws of genetics, nor would his work be known until the early twentieth century, long after his death. But it was known that pollen from one species in a given genus, if used to fertilize another species or a cultivated variety, could produce offspring that resembled neither parent exactly. Roses were one of the first important ornamental plants on which this wizardry was exercised, and this experimental tinkering produced on an enormous scale a change in the relation of the human race to the plants we grow. No longer was it "Nature or Nature's God," in Thomas Jefferson's phrase, to which we owed the diversity of the garden. We now had our own hand in the game.

At Parc Floral d'Apremont, the starred clematis accents the rounded rose.

In the explosion of roses after the four studs arrived in Europe, no one played a larger role than the empress Joséphine, whose given name was Marie Joséphine Rose and who was called Rose until she was crowned by her husband, Napoleon I, in 1804. No one before her did more to spur on the widespread planting of roses or to encourage the development of new roses and no one has matched her since. Shortly after she and Napoleon acquired Malmaison very late in the eighteenth century, Joséphine was gripped by a passion for roses that was surely one of the great horticultural love affairs of all time. From English nurseries she ordered the various China roses in whose genes lay the possibilities for extended or repeated bloom. Even though England and France were at war with one another, and though the English generally had the coast of France under blockade, it was for Joséphine a period of "the peace of roses": the English

Albertine has surprisingly large flowers for a wichuraiana hybrid and as well produces an amazing display every year.

THE GLORY OF ROSES

nurseryman John Kennedy was permitted unimpeded passage back and forth across the Channel to deliver great quantities of roses to Malmaison. By 1814 Joséphine's collection of roses numbered some 242 cultivated varieties of all types—gallicas, musks, damasks, and the rest—in addition to at least eleven species, some quite recently collected in the Orient. (It is worthy of remark that after Napoleon's marriage to Joséphine was annulled and Marie Louise of Austria became his new empress, Marie Louise had a rose named for her. So did Napoleon, although British nurseries renamed it Madness of Corsica. And Joséphine, unjustly, got her rose only posthumously, three decades after her death, when Imperatrice Josephine was introduced.)

The influence of the empress Joséphine on the breeding of new roses in France—based on the genetic treasures she assembled at Malmaison

Golden Wings is a favorite landscape rose, blossoming early in the season and sweetly scenting the garden until fall.

and made available to nurserymen—can be grasped by comparing her number of roses listed in the catalogs of two leading French nurseries. In 1791, one offered just twenty-five; in 1829, the number appearing in another was a staggering 2,562. This represents more than a hundredfold increase in just thirty-eight years. But this oft-told statistic requires some interpretation: by far the greater number of these roses has fallen into extinction, rescued from complete oblivion only by the listing of their names in such nursery catalogs. The sudden flood of new roses available to gardeners in the middle of the nineteenth century reflects the reigning passion of the day for floral novelties on the part of the public and the willingness of nurserymen to accommodate this passion. The idea that new roses should be carefully tested and indifferent or inferior ones rogued out and destroyed, not named and introduced, had not yet arrived.

In its color and bouquet, the Brandy hybrid tea rose reflects the sophisticated allure of such liquors as Armagnac and Courvoisier. OVERLEAF: *Floribunda roses spring from a mixed ancestry of full blooms and long flowering season; here the floribunda rose Westlander is at its peak of form and color.*

Malmaison fell into a shambles soon after Joséphine's death in 1814—one of many unhappy examples of gardens that do not long survive the person who made and loved them. But her house and her rose garden were restored early in the twentieth century as one of the major shrines for those who love the flowers she worshiped. And even if her garden had been allowed to pass into history and into ruin, her passion for roses would have lived on in Pierre Joseph Redouté's watercolor prints, *Les roses*, published between 1817 and 1824. *Les roses* was produced after Joséphine's collection of roses at Malmaison had already largely vanished or been vandalized, but Redouté painted many of the plants the empress had grown from 1803 on, and there can be little doubt of her influence in all of his later paintings and prints of roses.

Not only have new varieties of roses been created, but also new classes of roses. For instance, the Bourbon roses—so named neither for the French

ABOVE: *A climbing rose grafted to form a weeping standard makes a spectacular centerpiece in this Maine garden.* OPPOSITE: *Even the curling petals of blossoms beginning to fade bestow sensuous delight.*

ABOVE: *The formal rose gardens at Bagatelle in Paris rely on geometric shapes, horizontals, and verticals for skeleton structure and the roses themselves for the enrichment of the lines.* OPPOSITE: *Hidden in a shrine of climbing red roses, a small statue watches over the garden.*

THE GLORY OF ROSES

royal house nor for the American whiskey, but for the Île de Bourbon in the Indian Ocean—resulted from a chance hybrid between Parsons' Pink China and the autumn damask rose, from southeastern Europe. This hybrid was imported to Paris, where breeders busied themselves further in expanding the race of Bourbon roses, producing such individually named garden varieties as Souvenir de la Malmaison and Mme Pierre Oger, both of which are still grown today.

Another distinct nineteenth-century class of roses originated in Charleston, South Carolina, where a plantation owner named John Champney (sometimes spelled Champneys) crossed Parsons' Pink China with *Rosa moschata*, a species known to have been brought to England from Spain early in the sixteenth century. Champney gave the resulting hybrid, named Champney's Pink Cluster, to Philippe Noisette who sent seeds to

At Mottisfont Abbey, Hampshire, Complicata grows in profusion; it serves as a shrub rose as well as a climber or even a hedge rose.

THE GLORY OF ROSES

his brother Louis in Paris. Louis Noisette kept hybridizing these plants, developing a group of vigorous climbers with recurrent bloom known as the Noisettes. Some of these, including Blush Noisette, Claire Jacquier, and Mme Alfred Carrière, are still grown and valued today. A Noisette especially beloved in the southern United States (it is too tender to survive much further north than Richmond, Virginia) is Maréchal Niel, an opulent deep yellow with elegant pointed buds and a heady fragrance that has been described as reminiscent of strawberries.

There is no room here to trace further the rich history of the development of the rose during the nineteenth century, nor need to, since such scholars as Allen Paterson and Gerd Krüssmann have told the story in great detail. It is perhaps sufficient to say that at the end of the eighteenth century most roses grown in Europe could be divided into

A hybrid of the Persian yellow rose, Lawrence Johnston is a fine early flowering climber that takes its name from the creator of Hidcote Manor's garden.

THE GLORY OF ROSES

gallic roses, centifolia roses, and damask roses, with some overlap among the groups. By 1869, fanciers of the rose could ponder not only Bourbon roses and Noisettes, but also Portlands, Ayrshires, hybrid musks, hybrid perpetuals, teas, hybrid teas, and other classes. Additional Asian species, such as *Rosa multiflora*, *Rosa wichuraiana*, and *Rosa rugosa*, were collected and imported to Europe to increase the gene pool and multiplied still further the bewildering numbers of roses from which to choose. They added in their turn still new classes of hybridized roses, the multifloras, the wichuraianas, and the rugosas.

Anyone who examines a nineteenth-century catalog of roses will find it at first sight appealing in its diversity of plants and its tidiness in sorting them all into groups. Here are the gallicas, there the Noisettes, over there the damasks, and so on, with many cultivars under each heading. But as early as 1847, even as the numbers of roses in each category proliferated, criticism of the usefulness of the system of classification was heard. In America in that year Samuel B. Parsons observed that it "may often be difficult to ascertain whether a rose is a Damask, a Provence, or a Hybrid China; but there can be no difficulty in ascertaining whether it is dwarf or climbing, whether it blooms once or more in the year, and whether the leaves are rough . . . or smooth." Parsons proposed a much simplified scheme, with three classes:

> I. Those that make distinct and separate periods of blooms throughout the season, as the Remontant Roses.
> II. Those that bloom continually, without any temporary cessation, as the Bourbon, China, &c.
> III. Those that bloom only once in the season, as the French and others.

Parsons was able to follow his own scheme since he owned a prominent nursery in Flushing, New York, that offered more than three thousand roses. His fellow nurseryman, Joseph Breck of Boston, also complained in

Only species roses will come true when grown from seed and the seeds of a pollinated rose are to be found in fleshy rose hips. OVERLEAF: *Rosa rugosa is a native of maritime sands in Japan and has made its home in similar soils throughout the temperate world, as here on the east coast of the United States.*

his book *The Flower Garden* (1851), that "on the subject of the Classification of Roses, there have been much difficulty and confusion." But the old system endured: gallicas, damasks, Noisettes, and all the rest.

There have been more recent critics, as well. In the fifteenth edition (1933) of his influential book *The English Flower Garden*, William Robinson wrote that the "attempted classification of roses into teas, hybrid perpetuals, etc. is confusing and not sound, as all these roses are hybrids." He asked that nursery catalogs offer simple alphabetical lists of good roses, "without following the absurd attempt at classification." He even recanted his use of these classifications in the first fourteen editions of his book, "thereby doing infinite harm in many ways by confusing people with a multitude of kinds."

Since Robinson wrote, there have been new schemes of horticultural classification proposed for roses. One sensible one starts off by dividing

A vision of the profusion possible from intensively cultivated modern roses; after this bloom may come further, though admittedly lesser, displays.

THE GLORY OF ROSES

roses into: (*a*) modern garden roses, bred after 1867 (when La France—the first hybrid tea—appeared, shifting public taste from the full-blown roses of the past to its high and pointed buds, its less-spreading flowers); (*b*) old garden roses (bred before 1867); and (*c*) wild or species roses. Each class is further divided into climbers or nonclimbers, and then those subclasses into reblooming and once-blooming kinds.

Parsons made sense. So did Robinson, and so does the clear and rational scheme just described. But the old categories linger. Some classes, like the Pernetianas, have disappeared from catalogs, but the albas, the damasks, the gallicas, and others endure. The old classification has poetry to it: Shakespeare, with his damask roses and his musks and his eglantines, would have been ruined by the rationalism and efficient good sense of Parsons, Robinson, and others who want true order, who don't believe in distinctions without difference, no matter how nice they sound.

This house engulfed in rambler roses takes on the quality of a fairy-tale dwelling.

THE GLORY OF ROSES

I side here not with the poets, but with the realists. My reason is that when it comes down to individual roses, the same rose may be described in one catalog as a damask, in another as an alba, and in a third as a gallica. It's as confusing as going to an automobile dealer and hearing the same car described as a Toyota, a Rolls-Royce, and a Buick.

The names of natural species of roses, whether they honor a person, indicate a habitat, or single out some especially notable trait, are given in Latin—regardless of the vernacular—and italicized. Hybrids, selected varieties or forms, and other roses that have originated under cultivation are known collectively as *cultivars*, a fairly ugly portmanteau word meaning cultivated varieties, as distinguished from botanical varieties, which are variations within a species that are not sufficiently distinct to warrant species status of their own. Their names, not in Latin but in any of several modern European languages, are bestowed on them by their breeders or

Roses in shades of orange were popular in the 1950s and mauves most recently; when combined, the rose's variety of colors can refresh the most meager of souls.

by people in the nursery business who hope that a good name will say to customers, "Buy me." These names, called *fancy names* or sometimes (quite oddly) *Christian names*, serve the primary function of keeping one rose distinct from another in the garden or in the nursery catalog. But they are marketing devices as well, meant to have attraction that will win over potential buyers.

I would estimate that the number of hybrid roses that have been bred and named since the early nineteenth century amounts to well over thirty thousand. (Fairly accurate records have been kept since 1899 when the American Rose Society was founded and began to keep track of cultivars registered with it.) Many of these, of course, have long since passed out of existence, but thousands remain and many hundreds can be purchased commercially, from specialized mail-order nurseries. The number of roses that have been bred and then destroyed for lack of merit when their first blossoms appeared is astronomical.

While Dorothy Perkins is typically a vigorous climber, this valiant plant exists among grasses and seeds as ground cover.

I love to study the very names of roses as they appear in lists and catalogs. Some names, in several different languages, are highly musical and poetic. Félicité et Perpétue, Maiden's Blush, Frühlingsmorgen—who could hear such names and not want to grow the roses that bear them?

Since the early nineteenth century, there have been several patterns or fashions in the names of roses. Names in French have predominated for the good and sufficient reason that French breeders and French nurseries, starting with Jean-Paul Vibert at the very outset of the period of rapid development, got a head start on horticulturists everywhere. It was not long before there were hybrids of British, German, and American origin, as well as significant work in New Zealand. But any list of the roses that were bred in the nineteenth and twentieth centuries speaks with a decidedly French accent.

The glorious abundance of color and form in Monet's garden at Giverny is enhanced by the perfection of such blossoms as this Mme Caroline Testout.

With the hybridization of new plants that could be vegetatively propagated, human beings could alter the natural order, bringing into being plants to suit their own fancies and tastes. It also meant that anyone who wished could name a plant to suit his pleasure, to flatter those he had reason to flatter, to honor those he wished to honor. Persons whose names are given to plants enjoy a kind of immortality, especially if the plants are widely grown and highly admired, for their names may be known long after they themselves have gone to earth.

Count Lelieur, an early French hybridizer, named one of his creations Rose Lelieur, after himself. There is more than a little hubris here; modesty would seem to require that a rose breeder do himself no such honor, but bestow it on others. Modesty would also suggest that someone who wants a rose named for him should keep quiet and merely hope that

Meg blooms in colors from buff to apricot and peach and in almost-single flowered simplicity. OVERLEAF: *The succulent leaves of sedums in this urn juxtapose their strange beauty with the lushness of modern roses to create a rare atmosphere.*

such a thing will happen. King Louis XVIII was not inclined to keep quiet and hope. In 1814, the year that the monarchy was restored in France, he offered the opinion that the erstwhile Rose Lelieur should be rebaptized Rose du Roi. The count complied and Rose du Roi it was. But not in England. There the same rose was grown as Lee's Crimson Perpetual.

Roses generally carry the same name from one country to the next, but not invariably, as the transformation of the French king's rose to Lee's rose bears witness. When World War I came along, Britons took such umbrage at obviously German names that the Battenberg family became the Mountbattens. As for the rose named for Frau Karl Druschki, English nurserymen swiftly started to sell it as Snow Queen; the French followed suit with Reine des Neiges and in the United States it became White

ABOVE: *Early morning sun is captured and released by the roses of Bagatelle in the Bois de Boulogne.* OPPOSITE: *American Pillar makes a brilliant show in its season, but is neither recurrent nor scented.*

American Beauty. The rose that is called Peace in the United States and Great Britain has no fewer than three aliases: in France, where it was hybridized in the late 1930s, it is Mme A. Meilland, in Italy it is Gioia, and in Germany, Gloria Dei.

There have been some clear patterns in the naming of roses ever since the number of roses began to grow dramatically in the early nineteenth century, each rose needing its own name to identify it and separate it from all the rest. One of the first patterns was to name roses for members of the French and English aristocracy. Lady Fitzgerald and the Duke of Choiseul thus both had their namesake roses. So did a Comte de Chambord and Prince Camille de Rohan. Queen Elizabeth and Princess Margaret both have had roses named for them—although it is worth noting that the plants have altogether different parents. The Duke of Windsor also had his rose, but a German breeder, not a British one, did him the honor.

A second pattern involves the use of names of cities. Grüss an Aachen, which in English roughly means "kindly regards to the city of Aachen," is a pale pink first introduced in 1909 and still highly valued in both Europe and the United States. Such "kindly regards" were also sent by German breeders to the cities of Berlin, Coburg, and Teplitz; they named roses for Kassel and Dortmund as well, albeit without the greeting. In France, Dijon has its Gloire de Dijon, its rose to match its mustard, although it's a soft pink blended with yellow. Several cities in England have had roses named in their honor: City of York, City of Norwich, and City of Leeds.

In another pattern, roses are christened to honor the celebrities of the rose world. A recent rose, Graham Thomas, is named for the best-known expert on roses in Great Britain today. Sam McGredy, a member of the fourth generation of a prominent family of rose breeders in Northern Ireland who now lives and works in New Zealand, gave the family names Paddy McGredy and Molly McGredy to two of his favorite creations.

Though most commercial cut roses lack a true perfume, the classic simplicity of a sheaf of them creates a stunning visual aesthetic.

THE GLORY OF ROSES

THE GLORY OF ROSES

Political leaders—and sometimes their spouses—have also been frequently honored. Abraham Lincoln gave his name to both Honest Abe and Mr. Lincoln. Herbert Hoover was similarly honored in 1930, just as the Great Depression got underway. One rose was named for Konrad Adenauer, and another for Reichspräsident von Hindenburg. Lady Bird Johnson has had her rose, as have Pat Nixon and Rosalynn Carter. Before Nancy Reagan came to the White House, when her husband was still California's governor, First Lady Nancy was named for her. Two years after his death, a rose was named for John F. Kennedy. Benjamin Franklin had to wait longer, until 1969.

The name of a rose sometimes provides insight into the larger social history of its day. The process of choosing names may be deliberate and canny, or it may be an unconscious expression of the *Zeitgeist*, but in either case it is very revealing of our souls. Better Times dates from 1934, and thus speaks of hope amid grim economic conditions. Radar (1952) recalls postwar dreams of better living through electronics in the wonderful world that modern technology was surely about to lay before us. Chrysler Imperial, introduced the same year, reminds us of our former love affair with tail-finned gas-guzzlers and our failure to recognize that petroleum was not an infinite resource. Indy 500 also testifies to our fascination with fast machines.

Since World War II, the names of roses have indicated a strong preoccupation with popular culture, its pastimes and celebrities (not heroes, exactly). One trend concerns itself with the world of fashion. A rose introduced in 1949 was in fact named Fashion. Since then roses have appeared bearing the names Christian Dior, Vogue, and Fashionette (whatever that word means). Alcoholic beverages have also been celebrated in roses such as Chablis, Brandy, Cocktail, Glenfiddich, Scotch Blend, White Lightnin', Champagne Cocktail, and Drambuie—which happens to be a sport, or mutation, of another rose called Whisky Mac.

Potted fuschias and marguerites at the foot of a climbing hybrid tea at Cranborne Manor, Dorset, give support to the rose's supremacy at these historic seventeenth-century gardens.

THE GLORY OF ROSES

The celebrities of the entertainment world have hardly been neglected, considering roses named Judy Garland (there is also one called Over the Rainbow), Maurice Chevalier, Satchmo, Cary Grant, Arlene Francis, Ginger Rogers, and even Dolly Parton. Elvis has not yet gotten his rose, but Graceland did in 1989. The Disney influence has been especially pronounced with Dopey, Doc, Sleepy, Hi-Ho, Prince Charming, Bambi, Jiminy Cricket, and Pinocchio. Vladimir Nabokov has thus far escaped being remembered with a rose, except that there is a Lolita.

I have no idea of the next true fad in the naming of roses, but considering the increasing role played in our lives by solid-state electronics I would not be at all surprised to open a rose catalog one January and find among its new offerings plants called Fax, Macintosh, Modem, and Hypercard. Among new miniature roses, there might be Microchip, Microsoft, and Microwave.

This brilliant modern floribunda in the Forum speaks eloquently to the rose as an ancient Roman sign of opulence.

THE GLORY OF ROSES

Although operatic divas Lily Pons, Helen Traubel, and Maria Callas have lent their names to roses and there are roses named for Handel and Mozart, for Goethe and Picasso, in general, high culture has not been mined for its yield of names. But perhaps there is a change in sight. Among the most interesting roses of the late twentieth century are those belonging to the new class called English roses, bred by the distinguished British hybridizer David Austin. Austin has successfully combined the lush opulence of nineteenth-century shrub roses with the range of colors found in the hybrid teas that have dominated since the Edwardian era. All of these cultivars in this genuinely new race of roses (that bids fair to be the most widely admired and grown in the first decades of the twenty-first century) take their names from the poetry of Chaucer and Shakespeare— Canterbury, The Nun, Troilus, Othello, Prospero. Austin has also given the world its first and probably its last rose named for a cough drop. One

The rose adorns stone, concrete, plaster, brick, and wood with equal beauty and grace.

THE GLORY OF ROSES

119

of his most splendid productions is called Fisherman's Friend, thanks to a charitable auction in which the right to name the rose was won by this company that manufactures lozenges for scratchy throats.

I have a firm feeling that except in the work of David Austin, the art of naming roses has declined throughout the years since World War II. I like the old names like La France, New Dawn, and Radiance. I like even better the roses named for women about whom I know just one thing: that they gave their names to roses. And I have a persistent fantasy that in a garden of old roses I might late one evening discover the women themselves returned to life for an hour or so, walking the paths among the roses, inhaling the perfume, and talking softly among themselves. I would love to eavesdrop on Lady Mary Fitzwilliam, Lucy Bertram, Marie de Blois, and Mme de la Roche-Lambert. But I can't quite work up the same enthusiasm for Dopey and Jiminy Cricket.

ABOVE: *In this corner of La Pietra, Italy, the rose adapts to an informality verging on carelessness.* OPPOSITE: *A striped Bourbon rose is paired with* Phlomis samia *at Hidcote Manor in Gloucestershire.*

THE GLORY OF ROSES

121

THE
USES OF
ROSES

The Rose is of exceeding greate use with us; for the Damaske Rose (besides the superexcellent sweete water it yieldeth being distilled, or the perfume of the leaves being dryed, serving to fill sweete bags) serveth to cause solublenesse of the body, made into a Syrupe, or preserved with Sugar moist, or dry candid. . . . The red Rose hath many Physicall uses much more than any other, serving for many sorts of compositions. . . . The white Rose is much used for the cooling of heate in the eyes. . . .

—JOHN PARKINSON, *Paradisi in Sole: Paradisus Terrestris* (1629)

MANY ANCIENT TRADITIONS agree that the rose is the queen of flowers. She was created as such by Aphrodite, or by Allah, or by other gods. She was enthroned by other flowers eager to be her subjects, deferent to her beauty and pleased that she should represent them all. In "The Parliament of Roses to Julia" the seventeenth-century poet Robert Herrick describes this election.

Then in that *Parly,* all those powers
Voted the Rose: the Queen of flowers.

The genus *Rosa,* indeed of noble lineage, is the most beautiful member of the Rosaceae family, a large and widespread botanical family that has been of great benefit and utility to the human race since the beginning of agriculture. Apples, cherries, peaches, pears, raspberries, almonds, and other members of this family—distinguished by pink or white five-petaled blossoms in late spring or early summer—are kin to the rose. From them we get a rich assortment of tasty and nutritious fruits, many of which can be dried or otherwise preserved as jams or jellies. Many yield juice for refreshing beverages, either fermented or unfermented. In the case of almonds we get a delicious nut which has long been prominent in the cuisines of the Mediterranean Basin. Indirectly, through the agency of

Potted rugosas and hybrid teas await purchase on a Parisian street. PRECEDING PAGE: *Rain-washed windows frame a bucket of roses.* PAGE 122: *Carefully pruned and tied in, a climbing rose reaches the eaves of the entrance court at Sissinghurst Castle, Kent.*

THE GLORY OF ROSES

honeybees, members of the rose family give us honey, the earliest sweetener. The woody members of the rose family provide sweet-smelling wood for cooking and for carpentry, though what we call rosewood comes from a tropical tree outside the family. Among higher plants, only the legume and grass families have had comparable importance over so long a history.

Other members of the family continue to be useful today, but most lovers of the rose would scorn any effort to reckon its value in terms of a utilitarian calculus. The beauty of the rose is sufficient, they would insist; or, if roses do have their uses, beauty remains primary. I largely agree, although the economic role played by roses and their by-products today is important in western Europe, in Bulgaria, and in the United States. Furthermore, the uses to which they once were put makes a fascinating story, beginning with their uses in medicine.

Roses will provide a view where there is none, and here in the Municipal Rose Garden in Rome, they provide a frame for the view that is unequalled.

THE GLORY OF ROSES

Medical writers of ancient Greece and Rome as well as French and English herbalists of the seventeenth century would be very surprised to visit a modern pharmacy and discover that roses no longer play any role in medicine. Many drugs are made of natural chemicals—or their synthetic versions—that have a botanical source. Aspirin is a chemical analogue of a substance originally extracted from willow bark. Digitalis, which still is used to treat certain kinds of heart disease, was first produced from the seeds of foxgloves. Reserpine, used in treating states of anxiety and hypertension, comes from the root of the herb *Rauwolfia serpentina*, long a traditional remedy in India for snake bite. Several drugs derived from the Madagascar periwinkle (*Catharanthus roseus*) in very recent times have been developed for treating Hodgkin's disease. Roses, however, are now completely missing from our medicine cabinets.

Young roses at the refreshment stand of Giverny echo the profusion of roses throughout Monet's famed garden. OVERLEAF: *Roses and cosmos combine in a high summer display.*

THE GLORY OF ROSES

The eleventh edition of *Taber's Cyclopedic Medical Dictionary* (1970) has but one rose entry. It is for rose water and lists its sole use as lending an agreeable fragrance to lotions. I remember as a child my mother having a little blue bottle of eye drops made from rose water, but it seems no longer to be manufactured. My local pharmacist could not think of a single medical product based on roses in any way. I thought I might do somewhat better finding a contemporary legacy of the rich history of the rose in treating disease and promoting physical well-being by browsing in a health-food store. All that I could find was a small jar of crystals made from sea salt, extracts of rose petals, and rose geranium whose label promised that half a cup dissolved in bath water would calm and soothe the heart and bring romance into my life.

The day of the rose in medicine may have come to its end, but it had a long run. In his *Natural History*, written in the first century A.D. and quoted here from a seventeenth-century translation by Philemon Hol-

Dried aromatic leaves and flower petals—including rose petals—combined with fixatives and spices such as cloves, mace, cinnamon, and coriander make up potpourri.

THE GLORY OF ROSES

land, Pliny the Elder claimed that the rose "hath medicinal virtues and serveth to many purposes in physick. It goes into emplastres and collyries or eye-salves, by reason of a certain subtle mordacities and penetrative quality it hath." Ashes of roses, furthermore, "serve to trim the haires of the eyebrows." The leaves of wild roses if "reduced into a liniment with bear's grease doth wonderfully make hair grow again." Pliny also reported that the root of the dog rose (*Rosa canina*) was a cure for hydrophobia and that this virtue had been revealed by the gods in a dream to a woman whose son was near death after having been bitten by a rabid dog.

The English herbalist Bartolomaeus Anglicus wrote of the rose in 1495 that "nother is so vertuous in medicine. Among all floures of the world the floure of the rose is cheyf . . . an wythstandeth and socouryth agenst many syknesses and evylles." In his famous, influential, and fascinating tome, *The Herball, or General History of Plants*, the Elizabethan barber-surgeon John Gerard was much more specific, claiming so many

At the Parfumerie Fragonard in Grasse, France, elegantly presented soaps contain a distant echo of damask roses.

THE GLORY OF ROSES

131

THE GLORY OF ROSES

132

medical virtues for roses that he seems almost to be describing modern antibiotics. In the second edition of his *Herball*, published posthumously in 1633, Gerard's assessment of the musk rose details both its culinary and medical aspects. "The leaves of the floures eaten in the mornings, in the manner of a sallad, with oile, vineger and pepper, or any other way according to the appetite and pleasure of them that shall eate it, purge very notably the belly of waterish and cholericke humors, and that mightily, yet without all perill or paine at all. . . ."

Gerard gave the following recipe for "syrup of roses" in sufficient detail that adventurous souls today might make their own batch.

Take two pound of Roses, the white ends cut away, put them to steepe or infuse in six pintes of warme water in an open vessell for the space of

ABOVE: *A clematis, rose and* Hydrangea petiolaris *share an English cottage wall.* OPPOSITE: *Young roses, whether in a commercial nursery or part of an amateur's breeding enterprise, signify the expectations of those who spend their lives working with the queen of flowers.* OVERLEAF: *In this Kentish churchyard beds of roses appear where typically gravestones might be expected.*

twelves houres; then straine them out, and put thereto the like quantitie of Roses, and warme the water again, so let it stand the like time; do thus foure or five times; and the end adde unto that liquor or infusion, foure pound of fine sugar in powder; then boyle it unto the forme of a syrrup, upon a gentle fire, continually stirring it untill it be cold; then straine it, and keepe it for your use, whereof may be taken in white wine, or other liquour, from one ounce unto two.

The resulting syrup was claimed to be good for "loosing, opening, and purging the belly," for "opening the stoppings of the liver," and for "the trembling of the heart," among other things. I make no medical recommendation, however. Gerard also thought that roses "bringeth sleep . . . through their sweet and fragrant smell."

ABOVE: *The orange cast to these roses is a reminder of* Rosa foetida persiana, *which brought to rose breeding a range of colors hitherto impossible to achieve.*
OPPOSITE: *While rose colors now extend from lavender to scarlet, yellow and flame-orange to blood red and pearl white, the true blue rose is as unlikely as ever to occur.*

THE GLORY OF ROSES

anonymously in 1906 in *Good Housekeeping* magazine, reminisced about the asceticism that pervaded this religious community.

Roses were planted along the sides of the road which ran through our village and were greatly admired by the passersby, but it was strongly impressed on us that a rose was useful, not ornamental. It was not intended to please us by its color or by its odor. Its mission was to be made into rosewater, and if we thought of it in any other way we were making an idol of it and thereby imperiling our souls. In order that we might not be tempted to fasten a rose on our dress or put it in water to keep, the rule was that the flower should be plucked with no stem at all. . . . This rosewater was sold, of course, and was used in the community to flavor apple pies. It was also kept in store at the infirmary, and although in those days no sick person was allowed to have a fresh flower to cheer him, he was welcome to a liberal supply of rosewater to bathe his aching head.

The stills await at the Parfumerie Fragonard in Grasse, France; two hundred pounds of damask rose petals picked just as the morning dew evaporates will produce one ounce of rose oil.

THE GLORY OF ROSES

THE GLORY OF ROSES

The Shakers and their rose water cure for headaches notwithstanding, the use of the rose as a source of medicine began to decline in the nineteenth century. The American nurseryman Samuel B. Parsons's delightful and highly readable classic *The Rose: Its History, Poetry, Culture, and Classification* heaped scorn on the heads of authors who attempted to make the medical value of the rose "as brilliant as its floral reputation." He was especially contemptuous of a German writer appropriately named Rosenberg, who, he wrote, made the flower "a specific in every disease, and even attributes to it supernatural virtues." Parsons himself devoted only four pages to the medical properties of roses. Obviously a partisan of the temperance movement, he rejected altogether the prescription of alcoholic tincture of roses. Syrup of roses, in his view, owed what laxative effect it had to senna and other ingredients with which it was com-

ABOVE: *Modern roses, while perhaps historically inaccurate, add color to the ancient Roman Forum and its evocation of commerce and civil life.* OPPOSITE: *This Dorothy Perkins sports a rustic quality not often given to the rose, a rich reminder of the rose's adaptability.*

THE GLORY OF ROSES

Rambler roses share a pergola with grape vines while below, heritage rose bushes accept their light shade.

pounded. He did hold that ointments made with rose water were good for treating inflammations of the eye, but otherwise he approved of only three recipes for medications based on roses. Vinegar of roses, prepared by infusing dried rose petals in distilled vinegar, was "valuable for head-aches," when drunk in small doses. Honey of roses, made by boiling rose petals briefly with small quantities of water and honey for immediate use, was "esteemed for sore throats, for ulcers in the mouth, and for anything that is benefited by the use of honey." Parsons also valued a conserve made by bruising together in a mortar equal weights of sugar and rose petals moistened with a small amount of rose water as "good for the treatment of all chronics and affections of the bowels." And he thought rose hips might be beneficial to eat.

This particular assertion was borne out in Great Britain during World War II when rose hips, which are extremely rich in vitamin C, were widely consumed to prevent scurvy when citrus fruits were virtually unavailable. The hips were generally made into a syrup by first removing

An effective, quintessential nosegay is made from sprays of roses and bits of ribbon.

---

the stems of one pound of them, then grinding them into a paste, covering the paste with water, and simmering it for an hour. The liquid was then strained, one-half pound of sugar was added, and the mixture was boiled until the sugar dissolved.

The contribution that rose hip syrup made to preventive medicine during the war serves as a reminder that roses once had a great many culinary uses. Few of these uses survive. I remember that my grandmother Lacy in Dallas used to make candied rose petals by dipping them in egg whites and sugar and placing them on waxed paper to dry. She also made dainty sandwiches of white bread, with the crust removed, spread with rose petals and butter. These little sandwiches were one of her favorite delicacies to serve when she invited the ladies of the Lakeside Browning Society for tea.

Rose water is still widely used in Arabic, Greek, Indian, Iranian, and Turkish cuisines, especially as a delicate flavoring for desserts and sweets. A traditional Turkish recipe for rose-petal jam calls for fresh petals to be gathered early in the morning, while the dew is still on them. As it is tough, the white part of each petal where it is attached to the calyx is trimmed away. One part rose petals, one part sugar, and one part water are simmered until thickened, when a bit of lemon juice is added, no doubt to perk up what otherwise would be insipid foodstuff. I have also seen a recipe for rose oil, in which three quarts of rose petals are simmered for an hour with a pint of peanut oil, then strained into a bottle and stored in a cool place. The recipe suggests that a few drops add an elusive and somewhat mysterious flavor to cookies.

I have tried none of these recipes and probably never will, but it is clear that people today are culinary pikers as regards roses compared to the ancient Romans. Pliny the Elder wrote in the first century A.D. that "many delicate and dainty dishes are served up at table, either covered and bestrewed with Rose leaves [meaning petals], or bedewed and smeared all over with their juice, which gives no harm to those viands, but give a

OVERLEAF: *At a villa near Florence, roses frame a pair of classical statues like the heraldic supporters of a coat of arms.*

THE GLORY OF ROSES

commendable taste thereto." One Roman recipe, from Marcus Apicius (80 B.C.–A.D. 40), called for pounding fresh rose petals in a mortar with broth, mixing with calf brains, eggs, wine, raisins, oil, and pepper, and then baking slowly. A later recipe, prepared in the thirteenth century for one of the kings of Sicily, sounds like an adaptation from Marcus Apicius. Rose petals were pounded together with egg yolks, the boiled brains of pigs and pigeons, olive oil, brandy, and wine, then baked. The recipe claims that when the cook removed the lid from the baking dish a delicious fragrance would waft through the dining hall, making the guests eager to enjoy the repast.

I confess it: these recipes sound utterly revolting to me. They make me bow down in gratitude to the Spanish for discovering the New World, with its maize and squashes, its tomatoes and peppers, and especially its potatoes, so that we can leave our roses in the garden and out of the kitchen and dine on more suitable fare.

The Romans used roses in other ways than in cooking and medicine, ways that have also gone out of fashion, and long ago. The kinds of roses they grew were few in number compared with the large numbers that have been hybridized since the early nineteenth century. But they grew roses in great profusion, and they used them very imaginatively and lavishly, to the extent that the rose virtually symbolizes the voluptuousness and luxuriance of Imperial Rome. Pliny described the common practice of young men of privilege wearing crowns and garlands of roses at festive banquets, their fragrance not only being pleasant but also thought to prevent the ill effects of overindulgence in wine. Rose petals were often strewn on the floors on these occasions.

Cleopatra was a keen strewer of roses as well. When she met Mark Antony, she gave a series of banquets in his honor. For one of them she ordered the floor covered eighteen inches deep in rose petals held down by

The wonderfully fragrant flowers of New Dawn, one of the best known ramblers, continue to blossom for weeks.

THE GLORY OF ROSES

netting. For his part the emperor Nero was as soft-hearted on roses as he was hardhearted toward the early Christians. When he walked the beach his retinue of servants cast roses at his feet. At some of his banquets huge numbers of rose petals were released from the ceiling, smothering his guests in their sweet fragrance and their silken texture; one piece of lore holds that the smothering was not always metaphorical. Also at Nero's banquets and those of other Romans, it was customary to suspend one rose above the dining table in tribute to Harpocrates, the god of silence— a virtue he had learned from keeping confidential the amorous adventures of his mother Venus. Guests were honor-bound to keep private everything that was said at these banquets—under the rose or *sub rosa*.

Some Roman moralists disapproved deeply of the luxurious habits that roses inspired in their fellow citizens. Cicero, writing against Verres,

The trellis tacked to the roof of this shingled outbuilding provides a framework for training the shoots of blush-pink New Dawn and other climbers.

a corrupt and tyrannical governor of Sicily, was contemptuous of his official's habit of traveling through his province "carried in a litter borne by eight men, in which he reposed, softly extended upon cushions made of transparent material and filled with roses of Malta, having in his hand a net of the finest linen, and equally full of these flowers, whose fragrance gratified his eager nostrils." Seneca was similarly stern in his judgment of a man named Smyrndiride, a Sybarite who slept on mattresses of rose petals but suffered from insomnia if even a single petal were crimped.

Among the Romans, roses were associated with death as well as with the life of luxury. They were often planted on or near tombs and the wealthy left wills providing for their maintenance and replacement if necessary. After Mark Antony was defeated at the Battle of Actium and before he committed suicide by stabbing himself with his sword, he made

This rambler's long, leafy growths are already clambering ahead of the current season's flowers and must be carefully managed to ensure next year's rich blossoming.

Cleopatra promise to cover his tomb with roses. Simpler folk trusted strangers to pay such homage to them after death: "Sparge, precor, Rosas supra mea busta, viator." On modest tombstones common inscriptions such as this beseeched passersby to strew roses on the graves.

Christians adapted pagan practices to their own usage with different interpretations of their meanings. Saint Jerome, the fourth-century Church father who translated the New Testament from Greek into Latin, wrote that "the ancients scattered roses over the urns of the deceased, and in their wills ordered that these flowers should adorn their graves, and should be renewed every year. . . . These modest flowers were emblematic of their grief. Our Christians were content to put a Rose among the ornaments of their graves, as the image of life."

Roses continued to have their funerary uses. When Charles Dickens died, his devoted readers lined his casket with roses, filled his open grave with them, and strewed them over his tomb for many years thereafter. In the American South, it is still customary for families of means to have a florist make a blanket of roses to cover the coffin of one of their members. Another custom there is that on Mother's Day a person whose mother is dead wears one white rose, whose mother is living, a red one.

Not all roses are fragrant, but many are. One must speak of their fragrance in the plural, not the singular, for they vary greatly in their notes and overtones. In one of the best books on fragrant plants ever written, *The Fragrant Path* (1932), the American garden writer Louise Beebe Wilder described "the true old Rose scent" as "the most exquisite and refreshing of all floral odours—pure, transparent, incomparable—an odour into which we may, so to speak, burrow deeply without finding anything coarse or bitter, in which we may touch bottom without losing our sense of exquisite pleasure." But in her further discussion of the scent of roses Wilder noted that particular roses had their own hints of other fragrances—violets, honey, ripe strawberry, mignonette, lemon, and gar-

Baskets of cut roses outside a restaurant in the perfume-manufacturing capital of Grasse attest to the town's appreciation of the flower's importance.

Restaurant
~
Galerie
Gourmande
Crêperie
Bretonne
CREPERIE
L'ETOILE
super
raclette!

denia, to name a few. In the American Rose Society's 1962 annual bulletin, N. F. Miller added to the list of scents nasturtium, clove, parsley, apple, lily of the valley, fern, moss, and even linseed oil. Fragrance is notoriously subjective and its perception varies from one person to another, but there is universal agreement that some roses smell very sweet and that their odors are not simple and straightforward, but complex and a bit mysterious.

It is agreed that fragrant roses, above every other flower except lavender, keep their scent long after their petals have withered, and also that they can impart it to other substances, particularly to liquids. The world of roses is, therefore, a world of potpourri, of rose water, of attar of roses, and of precious and costly perfumes.

Potpourri—the pretty name, alas, means "rotten pot" in French—seems to have been first concocted in Elizabethan times, though it may

The nobility of the rose duly frames the nobility of classical statuary in the heart of the Italian countryside.

have been earlier. One of the most delightful of all experiences is to be a houseguest of someone who makes potpourri. One may find a jar of it on the bed table, open the lid, and inhale the fragrance of roses of a bygone summer mixed with such other scents as lavender and rosemary. The summer need not have been a recent one. I have a close friend who owns and runs a nursery and who in ten years has not had the time to make potpourri. But when opened, the glass and pottery jars scattered throughout her house still release a delicious and heady scent.

I am sometimes seized with the longing to be able to travel back through time and visit the gardens of those who have long since gone to earth, but who left records of them in their writings. I would like to visit Celia Thaxter's little garden of annuals on the Isle of Appledore, off the coast of southern Maine, and see what she called in her classic book *An Island Garden* (1894) her "sweet plot." I would like to walk the grounds of Monticello, and listen to Thomas Jefferson praise his pecans and speak of his charmingly foolish dreams of growing oranges in Virginia. And of course I would like to visit Gertrude Jekyll at her garden, Munstead Wood, in Surrey, the day she made potpourri.

In her book *Home and Garden* (1900), she described the process at great length. First, over many months, she gathered rose petals, bushels of them at once, picked early in the morning as soon as the dew had evaporated. They were spread out in a thin layer on cloths in a cool, dry place, allowed to dry slightly more, and then packed into jars with salt to keep them from molding and to retain their remaining moisture. Sweet geranium leaves were also gathered and similarly preserved, as were the flowers of lavender and the peels of Seville oranges stuck thickly with cloves. On the day the potpourri was made, late in summer, the contents of all the jars— amounting to a dozen bushels—were dumped on a brick floor by the studio hearth. Friends and their children were invited to help assemble the ingredients, with others such as mace, ground cloves, allspice, benzoin, and a compound of orrisroot called Atkinson's Violet Powder. With pokers and little shovels, the makers of potpourri stirred and turned and prodded the pile until at last, just before dusk, they stored it all in a wooden cask holding more than fifteen gallons. Then Jekyll and her guests would wipe

their feet and go inside her house for tea, leaving the mess they left behind for the charwoman to clean up the next morning.

In potpourri, the fragrance of roses comes from their preserved petals, melded with other ingredients. Rose water, however, as well as the attar of roses and essential oil of roses used in the making of perfume, takes its fragrance from fresh roses that are afterwards discarded. The Romans—according to Pliny's testimony, once again—referred to both rose water and oil of roses, but these substances were almost certainly weak tinctures of rose petals merely soaked in water or oil. Rose water as we use the term today is a highly distilled tincture of roses processed to strengthen and concentrate the scent. Accounts vary, as they always do in horticultural history prior to the early nineteenth century, but it is a fair guess that the technique of distilling rose water originated in Moorish Spain in the tenth or eleventh century A.D. and then spread eastward through North Africa, Turkey, Persia, and India.

A proud display of the ancient European species Rosa canina, *or dog rose, adorns the cathedral at Hildesheim, Switzerland.*

Rose water soon became a culinary ingredient. It was also used in finger bowls before and after a feast. And it served to purify Islamic mosques that had been defiled by Christian intrusions. When Saladin recaptured Jerusalem from the Crusaders in 1187, he ordered that the Mosque of Omar, which had been used as a church, be cleansed with rose water, brought from Damascus in a caravan of five hundred camels. When Mohammed II captured Constantinople in 1453 he converted the Byzantine church Hagia Sophia into a mosque after a similar purification.

Far more potent and far more costly than rose water is attar of roses. As is often the case with plants and their uses in olden times, historical accounts vary in regard to the time and the place of attar's origin. Sometimes it is held to have been manufactured in Constantinople at least as early as the fourteenth century and probably earlier. I prefer the much more romantic and often repeated story that it originated in early-seventeenth century India, in Shalimar, one of several gardens built by the

In this Italian candlelit niche, lilies and roses claim their traditional association with the Madonna.

THE GLORY OF ROSES

Mogul emperor Jahangir in Kashmir. There the emperor was fond of boating with one of his wives, the Persian-born Nur Jahan, in a canal filled with rose water. One morning she discovered a greenish froth floating on the water which turned out to be the concentrated essential oil of roses, distilled naturally by the sun's heat. She named the substance *Attar-i-Jahangire*, "the perfume of Jahangir." Delighted by the intense fragrance, the emperor ordered the deliberate manufacture of attar in large wooden casks subjected to the hot days and cool nights to produce by artifice what his wife had discovered by accident. (A rival story has the empress sitting in a bathtub of rose water in her garden, but I like the idea of the canal.)

The manufacture of attar of roses, dominated in the twentieth century by Bulgaria, has been carried on in India since the time of Jahangir and Nur Jahan. In 1842, an Englishman named Dr. Jackson published in

ABOVE: *A miscellany of roses in a crackle-glazed teapot sports that perfect balance of elegance and familiarity which sets the rose apart.* OPPOSITE: *Rose heps, or hips, can be spherical or bottle-shaped, as large as salad tomatoes or as small as peas, and they have a sweet, fleshy coat, but bristly seeds inside.*

THE GLORY OF ROSES

The Bengal Dispensatory an account of the process, which began right after dawn, when hundreds of men, women, and children gathered petals in sacks to take to the distillery.

> To procure the attar, the Roses are put into the still, and the water passes over gradually, as in the Rose-water process. After the whole has come over, the Rose-water is placed in a large metal basin, which is covered with wetted muslin, tied over to prevent insects or dust getting into it: this vessel is let into the ground about two feet, which has been previously wetted with water, and it is allowed to remain quiet during the whole night. The Attar is always made at the beginning of the season, when the nights are cool: in the morning, early, the little film of Attar, which is formed upon the surface of the Rose-water during the night, is removed by means of a feather, and it is then placed in a small phial; and day after day, as the collection is made, it is placed for a short period in the sun; and after a sufficient quantity has been procured, it is poured off clear, and of the color of amber, into small phials. Pure attar, when it has been removed only three or four days, has a pale greenish hue: by keeping, it soon loses this, and in a few weeks' time becomes of a pale yellow.

Attar, now often adulterated by rose geranium oil, is only one of the essential oils of roses used in making perfumes. Rose oils produced by enfleurage and extraction are much less expensive and exact. While attar generally comes from Bulgaria, India, and the Middle East, rose oil produced by enfleurage is more common in the south of France, the perfume capital of the world. To create rose oil by enfleurage, animal fats are spread on glass plates and layers of flower petals pressed into the fat repeatedly until their oils are absorbed. The oils are then extracted by mixing the fat with alcohol and heating. The oils dissolve in the alcohol and then rise to the surface for skimming.

Perfume makers guard their formulas and lists of ingredients as closely as possible and would never dream of mentioning in their advertisements that lard and other animal fats are part of the manufacture of

Roses crowd around a simple seat at Sezincote, a unique country house in Gloucestershire.

their costly wares—but a friend with a sensitive nose tells me that she detects a hint of roses in Arpège, Chanel No. 5, Joy, White Linen—and, very appropriately, in Shalimar.

By venturing into the manufacture of perfumes we have left behind any pure and unsullied consideration of roses solely as objects of great beauty and appeal. Roses contribute not a little to the world's economy. In fact, were some evil demon able to snap his fingers and thereby cause every last rose plant in the world to disappear, it would be a financial catastrophe of international proportions. Many, many people earn their decent livelihoods from roses, in a multitude of ways. From the workers who pick rose petals for attar in Bulgaria and those who pick them for distilled rose water in the fields in southern France to the perfume-counter clerks at Macy's or Lord & Taylor, the fragrance of roses means money.

This perfectly formed bloom is protected so that every sepal, every petal remains free of blemish in hopes of a prize on the show table.

In America between thirty- and fifty-million hybrid tea roses are sold every year by mail-order nurseries and local garden centers, the number varying according to the size of the crop in the fields of large wholesale growers and according to consumer demand. This estimate does not include climbing roses, miniature roses, shrub roses, or roses grown for the cut flower trade. At an average retail price of $10, the lower estimate of hybrid teas sold in the United States yields a figure of $300 million a year, quite a considerable figure.

The economic value of a rose, however, goes far beyond its retail purchase price. Of all ornamental plants, roses—especially hybrid teas—require the highest degree of maintenance, which, in turn, requires a great many accoutrements. Hybrid teas must be pruned back sharply and properly in late winter or very early spring. The enemies of roses are legion: aphids, sawfly caterpillars, Japanese beetles, leafhoppers, nema-

Dame's violet, oriental poppies, snapdragons, and irises combine with roses to make a millefiori *tapestry in Monet's gardens at Giverny.*

todes, and spider mites are only a few of the long list of creatures out to get them. Bacterial infections can cause crown gall outbreaks. Rust diseases, mildews, and black spot disease all disfigure foliage and weaken plants, leaving them susceptible to further ailments. And if many roses are grown in close proximity in a small garden, the garden becomes a monoculture, resembling the agricultural monocultures of potatoes in Ireland in the early nineteenth century and cotton fields in the American South in the 1920s and 1930s. In a monoculture diseases spread easily and insect populations especially fond of that one kind of plant explode. Unless they are of the strict organic persuasion, gardeners who wish to bring the insects' feast to a speedy conclusion will fill their sheds with insecticides such as carbaryl, malathion, and rotenone. They will also want fungicides

ABOVE: *In the midst of an extraordinary profusion of blossom a gardener continually works at deadheading in order to maintain the display.* OPPOSITE: *The ease of cultivation and certainty of performance has kept American Pillar a rose of popular choice since its introduction in 1909.*

THE GLORY OF ROSES

Introduced in 1900, the elegant but scentless white Frau Karl Druschki is one of the earliest of its class still commonly grown.

on hand when they first glimpse black spot or mildew. Dedicated home rose growers will need pocket pruners, spraying devices, leaf-and-thorn strippers, hoses, and irrigation systems. They may want trellises and arbors and arches. If they are prudent they will want protective gloves of sheepskin. Furthermore, roses are heavy feeders, generally requiring regular applications of dried manure or chemical fertilizers. They may need mulching with pine bark or cocoa hulls. Therefore, the more roses that are grown, the greater the profits in the chemical and tool-manufacturing industries.

There is also money to be made by breeding new roses. This business much resembles looking for needles in haystacks, except that needle-searchers have no chance of making a living at their craft and professional hybridizers have a slim one. Here are the odds of the profession. Out of two thousand seeds sown from a particular cross, about ten percent will

Beauty in need of restoration, but beauty still: hard pruning and good feeding will dispel the thin, twiggy growth and poor foliage.

THE GLORY OF ROSES

not germinate. Of those that do, up to twenty-five percent may be albinos, incapable of photosynthesis and survival. If there is even one keeper in the remaining batch—one whose first flower, produced when the plant is only a few inches tall, appears worthy of further scrutiny and evaluation—the hybridizer is lucky.

The criteria for judging roses for introduction into the nursery trade are rigorous. The color must be appealing, first to the breeder, then to whatever tastes are in fashion among the gardening public. (Hot shades of orange were in vogue in the 1950s, and smoky mauves have been popular in the last decade or so.) Fragrance is desirable, although this particular criterion is so often given short shrift that complaints about scentless roses are common. Foliage color should be a rich, deep green. Disease resistance must be heeded, although susceptibility to black spot or mildew sometimes doesn't show up until well after a rose has been propagated in large quantities, named, and formally introduced. Finally, the new rose should

Hard-pruned in winter to a strong bud, the new growths respond to the first warmth of spring.

THE GLORY OF ROSES

have the elusive quality of distinctiveness, a visible difference from any other rose on the market.

A blue rose, if one ever turned up, would be a rose of rare distinction. The hybridizer who looked over a batch of seedlings one morning and discovered that one of them bore flowers as blue as lapis lazuli or sapphires would make a very considerable fortune. There are some tales told of blue roses. The nineteenth-century British rosarian William Paul referred in his book *The Rose Garden* (1848) to legends that the Moors in Spain had blue roses, said to have been "obtained by watering the plants with indigo water." Paul was highly dubious of this claim: "That they had such cannot for a moment be supposed; and the means by which it has been said that they obtained them is still more questionable." In the lore of the blue rose,

ABOVE: *Under the wide sky, reflected in a garden pool, a high yew hedge protects these roses from winds sweeping across the Weald of Kent.* OPPOSITE: *The bounty of Field Farm in Kent: myriad roses, including the wonderfully striped Rosa Mundi.* OVERLEAF: *The celebrated Parisian rose garden at Bagatelle was begun in 1903 on the site of a riding paddock used by the sons of Napoleon III.*

THE GLORY OF ROSES

another rumor has it that a hybridizer in Ulster did discover one among his seedlings but destroyed it immediately for fear that this novelty would ruin people's sense of good taste.

One year before Paul's book appeared, Samuel B. Parsons, in the United States, opined in his book *The Rose* that if ever blue roses existed they had passed into extinction. But he was optimistic that science and technology might one day produce them. Blue roses, in his view, would be a "singular result," and "well worth the trial." He then went on to write:

> Ten years ago, the man who should have foretold that the flickering shadow would be made to stand still, and that intelligence would be sent a thousand miles with the quickness of the lightning's flash, would have subjected himself to the strongest ridicule; yet these results have both been obtained—one by Daguerre, and the other by one of our own countrymen. . . . After the invention of the Daguerreotype and the Magnetic Telegraph, nothing can be deemed impossible or incredible,

A simple larch wood frame supports a climbing rose at Mottisfont Abbey; centaurea and lamb's ears provide complement and other herbaceous plantings lend interest when the roses are gone.

THE GLORY OF ROSES

respecting the natural agents which have been placed by Supreme Wisdom in the hands of man.

There are no blue roses yet because the genus *Rosa* lacks entirely the gene governing the production of delphinidin and other pigments responsible for flowers that are blue. And perhaps there never will be a blue rose. But Samuel Parsons's sunny view that "nothing should be deemed incredible," including blue roses, may be correct considering the recent technology in genetic engineering and the ability to give plants borrowed genes. The economic value of the first blue rose—I am not so sure about its aesthetic value—would be vast indeed.

The investment of energy, time, and money required to develop a new rose, even if not a blue one, is enormous. But the profits a highly successful rose can earn for its breeder and for many other people as well are considerable. Mass propagation by budding—inserting a vegetative

The abundance of vivid hybrid teas, floribundas, and polyantha roses make a stately show not found in most private gardens.

THE GLORY OF ROSES

growth bud onto an understock that provides a well-established root system—means that one plant can in just three or four years be turned into hundreds of thousands of clones, or genetically identical plants. An international patent system for plants means that for seventeen years after a rose is introduced, its hybridizers or the firm they work for receives a fee for each plant propagated and sold by commercial nurseries.

Even people who don't grow roses themselves may have roses as cut flowers 365 days a year, for their own personal pleasure in indoor arrangements or for giving to friends, relatives, and lovers. We tend, I think, to take our local florist shops for granted, as pleasant places with helpful and generally very nice salespeople and with fresh roses and other flowers always available under refrigeration. We say we bought some roses from

ABOVE: *New Dawn, a sport of Dr. Van Fleet, is one of the most popular of all climbing roses and with good reason as here it creates the scene for a lovely garden seat.* OPPOSITE: *Golden rosebuds ready for market in Paris continue the many traditions of giving flowers: the presentation of a yellow rose once conveyed the message, "Let us forget."*

THE GLORY OF ROSES

the florist, without thinking where they came from or without realizing that they may have traveled very long distances indeed—from Mexico, or the Dominican Republic, but most likely from Holland.

A few years ago I visited the cut flower auction warehouse at Aalsmeer in the Netherlands, which is run by a cooperative of more than four thousand Dutch growers. Its customers are a corresponding number of professional buyers and brokers. At this three-hundred-thousand-square-meter warehouse, in five separate auction rooms, nine million cut flowers are sold every day between 4:30 A.M. and noon. One auction room, where the brokers sit at tables on steeply tiered floors, electronic buttons in front of them to make bids via a computer, is devoted solely to roses. As the auction proceeds, one trolley after another reaches the floor, each containing 2,760 roses in twelve carefully packed containers, worth well over four thousand dollars retail for top grade stems. Each trolley

ABOVE: *From such simplicity as found in this delicate dog rose, all modern roses derived: five sepals and five petals enclose a boss of yellow stamens with stigmas in the center.* OPPOSITE: *One reason for New Dawn's incessant popularity is that sprays of its blush pink flowers continue until fall.*

THE GLORY OF ROSES

THE GLORY OF ROSES

180

pauses for only a few seconds as bids are offered and then the central computer sends it off along a complex network of tracks to the area where the successful bidder's refrigerated truck is parked. A rose that was harvested on Monday and auctioned on Tuesday may be in a European florist shop by Wednesday afternoon. Those roses bought at Aalsmeer for the U.S. market leave the Amsterdam airport by jet in early afternoon for several American cities. Most of them will have reached florist shops within thirty-six hours after they were sold.

People who give their lovers one dozen long-stemmed red roses on a birthday or on Saint Valentine's Day may have nothing in mind beyond expressing a fond sentiment with a gift of brief beauty. But greenhouse workers and owners, truck drivers, waiters in the Aalsmeer auction house restaurant, brokers, airline pilots, jobbers, and florists both wholesale and retail—all of these people and more find in someone's sentimental gift of roses a purely practical benefit.

ABOVE: *This bold climbing rose on a Nantucket fence intimates the pleasures of the garden within.* OPPOSITE: *Tin cans set among this tumble of summer flowers are traps for earwigs.*

THE GLORY OF ROSES

THE
MEANINGS
OF ROSES

Poetry is lavish of roses; it heaps them into beds, weaves them into crowns,
twines them with the goblet used in the festivals of Bacchus, plants them in the
bosom of beauty—nay, not only delights in the rose itself upon every occasion,
but seizes each particular beauty it possesses as an object of comparison to the
loveliest works of nature—as soft as a rose-leaf; as sweet as a rose; rosy clouds;
rosy cheeks; rosy lips; rosy blushes; rosy dawns, &c., &c.

—Unidentified writer, quoted in JOSEPH BRECK, *The Flower Garden* (1851)

HOW DID ROSES come to be?
Why are some of them white, others red, and still others yellow? Why do
most roses have thorns, sometimes very formidable ones? Today we seek
the answers to these and other questions about roses—or any plants—
through biological science. The answers lie in evolution within the plant
kingdom, in chromosomes and genes, in the coevolution of plants with
their insect and other pollinators, and in their need for protection from
injury by animals. But these particular kinds of answers have originated
only comparatively recently, in sciences that deal not with meanings but
with functions, not in *why* but in *how*. For most of the history of our life
together with roses, we have seen them as symbols, and very powerful
ones indeed. "Roses must *mean* something," we have thought, and then
gone in quest of these meanings.

Human beings have been defined in various ways—as rational animals, featherless bipeds, and tool-using animals, among other definitions.
But we are primarily symbol-using creatures. Our most important tool of
all is the symbol. We live in a social, political, and personal world that we
have fashioned out of symbols that are basically highly arbitrary. There is
no intrinsic reason that a red traffic light should mean stop and a green one

Cranborne Manor, Dorset, once a hunting lodge of King John, maintains this box-
wood garden graciously accented with climbing roses. PRECEDING PAGE: *A*
vast dog rose, purportedly a thousand years old, reaches the eaves of Hildesheim's ca-
thedral. PAGE 182: *A tightly closed bud nestles amid heavy-petalled blooms.*

THE GLORY OF ROSES

185

should mean keep going. There is no reason that the four letters that spell the word tree in English or the sounds we utter when we say that word should mean tree—nor that *Baum* in German, four different letters and a different sound altogether, should mean the same thing. It has often been noted that when a word is repeated over and over, it loses meaning: its arbitrary nature stands suddenly revealed. But our symbolic character goes far beyond the construction of a meaningful world out of arbitrary marks and arbitrary sounds. We want to find in the non-human world of natural objects meanings as well. We want nature to speak to us, to teach us lessons, to tell us things. We even want to believe that human actions—and the actions of gods that often are amazingly like us—have brought into being parts of the natural order, such as plants.

Of all the plants that have grown in gardens in lands around the

At Mottisfont Abbey, Hampshire, boxwood and Irish yews are the dramatic bare bones of a rose garden in winter. PRECEDING PAGE: *A climbing wreath of roses covers this exterior in Bracciano, Italy.*

THE GLORY OF ROSES

Mediterranean Sea since the earliest days of classical antiquity, the rose has qualities that suit it most perfectly for symbolic interpretation. It has surpassing beauty of form, ranging from the simplicity of *Rosa canina*, with its five petals, to the double forms of *Rosa gallica* and its natural hybrids that have appeared from spontaneous mutation or accidental crossing with other species. White and red, the two most common colors in those species of the rose native to Europe and Asia Minor, fit easily into the vocabulary of symbolism that takes white to be an emblem of innocence and purity, red to be a token of passion and of blood. Not all roses have scent, but many have strong, sweet fragrance that endures even after the flowers wither and the petals fade. Many roses open from tight and pointed buds into full-blown flowers, suggesting a promise and then its fulfillment—or an innocence that changes to something quite other, with

Cottage-garden flowers surround a wayside chapel in Italy.

THE GLORY OF ROSES

189

maturity and experience. The flowers of roses are soft to the touch, but the plants that bear them often also bear thorns so sharp and vicious that they may pierce skin and wound to the point of bloodshed. It is a flower that inspires love, but that also may inflict pain. There is nothing insipid about it at all.

The rose looms large in Greek and Roman myth and legend. For the Greeks, it was preeminently the flower of the goddess of love, Aphrodite, believed to have sprung from the sea foam attending her birth from the salty waters of the Mediterranean. For a time, all roses were white, but when Aphrodite's handsome lover Adonis was mortally wounded by a boar while hunting, red roses entered the world. One tradition has it that his blood stained the nearby roses and turned them red. Another claims that in her haste to reach her stricken lover, Aphrodite was pricked by the thorns of a white rose, and that it was her blood that turned it red. In

This rose, which might otherwise captivate merely for its velvety pink petals, is given a special luminescence by its spreading golden center.

THE GLORY OF ROSES

Roman mythology the tale has other variants. Cupid, the son of Venus (the Roman equivalent of Aphrodite), spilled a cup of wine on some roses in a tipsy moment, changing them from white to red. On another occasion, annoyed after a bee stung him while he was sniffing roses, he shot an arrow into the plant, thus endowing it with sharp thorns.

Persian lore tells another tale, not of goddesses but of the first nightingale. Wanting to keep awake to sweeten the cooling night air with its melodious songs, it pressed itself against the thorns of a rose in a garden. This ingenious way of inducing insomnia succeeded, but the bird wounded its chest slightly, and the morning after it first sang to the delight of humans, the white roses where it had perched had changed to red.

Ordinary mortals, albeit illustrious ones, are also credited with bringing the rose into being, through one of those metamorphoses of which Greco-Roman culture was so fond—those transformations of nymphs and human beings into trees or flowers. The best example is a

The bright, double-flowered Fellemberg is also known as La Belle Marseillaise.

THE GLORY OF ROSES

A variety of climbing roses scale the renaissance façade of La Pietra, Italy, grounded by pots of marguerites.

Queen of Corinth named Rhodanthe. (I find the story suspicious not just because of its fabulous burden of content, but also because her name means "rose flower.") Pursued by overeager suitors, she took refuge in a temple of Diana, with her subjects outside the portico to protect her. In their love for their queen, they chanted that she should be made a goddess. Apollo, Diana's brother, overheard the chant and, zealous to preserve his sister's territory, changed Rhodanthe into a rosebush. He made a few other changes as well, while he was at it. Her suitors became caterpillars, bees, and butterflies—all forms of life still apt to be seen pursuing the good things that roses offer them. Her subjects, in order to guard her still, became thorns.

In the vast literature devoted to roses since the nineteenth century, it is commonly said that the flower's associations with Aphrodite, with

The contrast of the rose's bright beauty against somber foliage evokes many traditions, such as covering the coffin of a loved one with a lush blanket of roses.

pagan sensuality, and with the official persecution of the early Christian church on the part of Nero and other rose-loving emperors brought about a Christian aversion to roses until the rise of the cult of the Virgin Mary in the ninth century or thereabouts. This claim would seem to be one of those stories that get passed on from one book to another, with little foundation in fact. The evidence, strongly to the contrary, is that roses play a large part in early Christian lore. The first-century theologian Saint Clement of Alexandria disliked the practice of wearing garlands of roses, but said nothing against the rose itself. As early as the fourth century A.D., Saint Ambrose found in red roses the symbol of the blood of martyrs and in their thorns the emblem of the sufferings they endured.

Stories about the lives of many martyrs and saints abound with roses. One of the earliest of these concerns Saint Cecilia, whose father

Narrow buds unfurling regularly hold sway over rounded blowsy roses in today's cut-flower fashion, making a full but tidy arrangement.

arranged that she should be married to a young Roman named Valerian. After the ceremony, in the privacy of her bridal chamber, she told her new husband that she had been visited by an angel, to whom she had vowed perpetual virginity. Valerian replied that he would believe her and respect her vow only if he too could see the angel. "Be baptized and become a Christian first," Cecilia said. Valerian complied, having himself baptized by the bishop of Rome, and on his return he found the angel by his wife's side placing a crown of white roses on her head. The angel then crowned Valerian with red roses. But this story does not end at this charming point.

Red roses, as Saint Ambrose said, betoken martyrdom. Valerian and his brother, who both became devout Christians, began to gather the corpses of their fellow believers who had been slain during the days of

Both the Cotswolds and the rose promise a fairy-tale quality and together, they never fail to ring true.

THE GLORY OF ROSES

persecution. For this good work they were themselves executed, and Cecilia herself was sentenced to death after she buried her husband and brother-in-law. The Roman authorities tried to suffocate her in her bathroom by building fires outside the door and the windows. Miraculously, Cecilia survived for days, singing all the while—the reason she is a patron saint of music. Finally she was beheaded, although legend holds that she afterward lived three more days, before finally shutting her eyes and going to her heavenly rest, to the place where angels sing and roses stay in eternal flower.

A later story with considerably less gore concerns Saint Elizabeth, queen of Hungary in the thirteenth century, who regularly fed the poor bread that she concealed in her apron in defiance of her husband's orders against such works of charity. On a bitter winter day when no flowers

At the Roseraie de l'Hay, there are a variety of designs each showing to perfection a style, type, or history of the rose and together affirming the rose's primacy in the garden.

were in bloom, the king discovered her on one of her errands of mercy. He flew into a rage and demanded to know what she was carrying. "Flowers," she lied to him in hope of avoiding his wrath, but he ripped her apron off. Out of it fell not loaves of bread but many dozens of roses, with beautiful glowing colors and a rich fragrance that perfumed the winter air.

But the chiefest symbolism of the roses in Christian thinking involves both Christ and the Virgin Mary, in associations that seem clearly to reflect elements of the more ancient mythology surrounding Adonis and Aphrodite.

According to Saint Bernard of Clairvaux, the five-petaled dog rose (*Rosa canina*) stood for the five wounds of Christ during his Crucifixion—the nails that pierced his hands and feet, the spear to his side. A variant on this interpretation makes the five petals stand for Christ's five senses in his

ABOVE: *At Parc Floral d'Apremont, near Nevers, this glimpse of a rose bush surrounded by lush green captures the romance of the unexpected and beautiful.*
OPPOSITE: *Roses old and new are not all there is to be seen at Sissinghurst Castle, Kent, a wonderful garden of traditions and innovations.*

THE GLORY OF ROSES

incarnation as a human being. Saint Albertus Magnus, a Scholastic theologian, stated that before Christ's death, all roses were white. Christ's blood, shed for the redemption of the human race, brought red roses into being. Another tradition holds that yellow roses also are due to Christ's passion, having been stained permanently by the rust of the iron nails that fixed him to the cross. As for the crown of thorns, some legends hold that it was made from the thorny stems of roses stripped of flowers, and that it was meant as the antithesis of the crowns of rose blossoms stripped of thorns worn by the Caesars.

The associations of roses with the Virgin Mary are even richer than those with Christ. Saint Ambrose wrote that the rose, alone among flowers, originated in heaven, not on earth. In heaven, it bore no thorns, but when Adam sinned it fell to earth, now equipped with sharp thorns to remind us painfully of our misdeeds and our transgressions, but still retaining great beauty and fragrance to give us hope of salvation and of the

The remarkable Mme Caroline Testout was fittingly named for a fashionable couturier in the late nineteenth century.

heavenly paradise. (Christ is, of course, also called the Second Adam.) A parallel legend holds that before the Fall, Eve kissed a rose in Eden, changing it from white to red. A variation holds that the rose was Eve's favorite flower, and that it was she who named it; it turned red when she was driven with Adam out of Eden. In later Christian piety, dating from the twelfth century Mary was called "the rose without thorns," because her Immaculate Conception kept her free of the original sin that is the common human lot. The white rose was the symbol of Mary's purity, the yellow rose of her wisdom, and the red rose of her sorrow during her son's Crucifixion. As Christian devotion to the Virgin continued to develop during the Middle Ages, Mary became ever more closely tied to legends involving roses. Paintings and altarpieces showed her sitting with the Infant Jesus in a garden, often a rose garden, enclosed by walls or hedges, an iconographic motif understood to mean her virginity. Depictions of the Assumption of the Virgin commonly show white lilies and red roses

The elegant rose in varying stages from tight bud to loose blossom gives ample justification for its constant acclaim. OVERLEAF: *When Sleeping Beauty pricked her finger and fell asleep, hedges of roses grew up around the castle walls and protected all within for one hundred years.*

THE GLORY OF ROSES

miraculously growing around her tomb, and scenes of her coronation in heaven use wreaths of full-blown roses as her crown.

But the highest point in the history of Christian thinking about the religious significance of the rose occurs not in stories about the saints nor in theology nor in popular piety nor in painting, but in poetry—near the conclusion of "Il Paradiso," the third part of his *Commedia*, where Dante reaches the end of his long journey through the worst and the best possibilities of human life. After losing his way in the "dark wood of error," Dante travels through the Inferno, inhabited by those human souls that have so separated themselves from God that they live on, throughout all eternity, without the faintest possibility of hope. Led by his fellow poet Virgil, who is one of the virtuous pagans consigned to Limbo and who

This colorful barrage of flowers gives support to the view that a variety of plants alongside the rose enhances rather than detracts from its beauty.

THE GLORY OF ROSES

stands for human reason, Dante finds his every sense assaulted by the noise of confusion, by the evidences of ever-increasing degrees of evil, and by muck and fire and ice. He then ascends to Purgatory, still led by Virgil, where he beholds the conditions of those souls who were deficient in love but who have the eventual hope of restoration to the presence of God. Near the end of "Il Purgatorio," Virgil departs and Dante is led through Paradise by Beatrice Portinari as the symbol of redeeming love.

The climactic moment in this wonderfully well-wrought masterpiece of late medieval literature comes in "Il Paradiso" when Dante ascends to the vision of a white rose, representing the Church as the Bride of Christ. Here angels swarm and fly like bees, alighting on the petals to rest and then plunging deeply into the heart of the rose for its sweet nectar. In wonder and amazement, Dante asks Beatrice to interpret the rose, but

Regardless of the weather, devotees of roses and Monet enjoy a stroll at Monet's recently restored garden at Giverny.

THE GLORY OF ROSES

she is unable to. The task falls to Saint Bernard of Clairvaux as a representative of the Christian contemplative life. Saint Bernard points out the souls of the blessed ones who sit upon the petals of the rose—of a redeemed Eve, of Rachel, of David, of saints Francis, Benedict, and Augustine, and Beatrice herself. Under Saint Bernard's guidance, Dante next embraces the vision of the Blessed Virgin, of the Holy Trinity, and of the Incarnation of God in Christ. He has come to the very presence of God, understood as an all-powerful love which moves the sun, the other heavenly bodies, and all creation as it was in the beginning and ever shall be, without ceasing in its holy power. It is this Mystic Rose which has drawn Dante upward, out of the dark wood of error and its sorry consequences, unto itself, unto salvation through the grace of God.

Dante's vision of the Mystic Rose has its architectural equivalent in the circular stone and stained-glass rose windows of Gothic cathedrals.

ABOVE: *For its perfection, the rose has often been called upon to be the symbol of beauty, wonder, and hope.* OPPOSITE: *An idyllic spot for visitors to Hidcote Manor, Gloucestershire, to sit among the roses.*

THE GLORY OF ROSES

Symbolizing God, eternity, and perpetual light, they also stood for the Virgin Mary. In 1912, in *Mont-Saint-Michel and Chartres*, Henry Adams wrote that the Gothic architect "felt the value of the rose in art, and perhaps still more in religion, for the rose was Mary's emblem. One is fairly sure that the great Chartres rose of the west front was put there to please her, since it was to be always before her eyes, the most conspicuous object she would see from the high altar. . . ."

The rose has been so inexhaustible in its meanings that its associations with Christ and with the Virgin never drove out other, much more human ties, even erotic ones. Heavenly love, or what the early, Greek-speaking Christians called *agape* (in Latin, *caritas*), never stands quite apart from the more frankly erotic love. During roughly the same period when Dante

At Spetchley Park, England, careful choice of plants ensures not only that flowering seasons overlap but that tall bearded irises thrive in the shade cast by the trained roses above.

was writing his *Commedia*, with its conclusion celebrating the Mystic Rose as the Church, another great poem was being written in the vernacular, although French rather than Italian. *The Romance of the Rose*, a composite work of some four thousand lines written in the early thirteenth century by Guillaume de Lorris plus another fourteen thousand lines written around 1280 by Jean de Meung, tells the allegorical tale of a lover making his way through a tangled maze of obstacles to the rose he seeks as the embodiment of perfection. Allegory and other layers of meaning and significance aside, the triumphant conclusion of the poem, describing the poet's overcoming his timidity to fulfill his quest, is overtly sexual, clear in its reference to the deflowering of a virgin. The poet grasps the rose bush in both his hands, but carefully avoiding the thorns. He plucks the bud, caresses the petals, and then opens them, to spill his own seed deep within

On a corner of Cranborne Manor, Dorset, unexpected ferns and moss provide a romantic backdrop for a tangle of climbing roses.

THE GLORY OF ROSES

the flower—which in its turn communicates to him its feeling of ecstasy and delight.

Little of the poetry that has been devoted to the rose is quite so explicitly sexual as the final lines of *The Romance of the Rose*. More often the poetry is merely amorous, and uses the rose as a means whereby a lover can praise the high merits, the beauty, and charm of the beloved. (The lover is always male, the beloved always female. Almost everywhere in the West, the rose is feminine; only in Arab culture, which holds that roses sprang sweetly from the sweat of Mohammed, is the rose considered to be masculine in character.) These lines from a poem written by Thomas Campion (1567–1620) are fairly typical of this love poetry:

There is a garden in her face,
Where roses and white lilies grow,
A heavenly paradise is that place,
Wherein all pleasant fruits do flow.

Careful consideration of hardiness, color, and season of flower in garden planting produces an effect that pleases the eye.

THE GLORY OF ROSES

The sentiments are human and secular, but they reflect some ancient religious traditions as well: Eve was thought to have named the rose in Eden and roses and white lilies grew on the sepulcher of the Virgin. Robert Burns, of course, meant to compliment his love by comparing her to a "red, red rose." And the second stanza of Ben Jonson's "Song: To Celia" suggests that Celia has the remarkable power of giving permanence to a wreath of ephemeral roses and of lending them a perfume of her own that is superior to theirs.

> I sent thee late a rosy wreath,
> Not so much honoring thee,
> As giving it a hope, that there
> It could not withered be.
> But thou thereon did'st only breathe.
> And sent'st it back to me;
> Since when it grows and smells, I swear,
> Not of itself but thee.

The sympathetic relation between nature and art is seen at Monet's garden in Giverny, where the fresh pastels of roses such as these mirror the painter's palette.

THE GLORY OF ROSES

But the message of the rose to the beloved is often one of ephemerality, of the urgency to seize on love, to express it before youth and beauty inevitably and all too quickly fade away. Edmund Spenser wrote in *The Faerie Queene* (1590):

Gather therefore the Rose, whilest yet is prime,
For soon comes age, that will her pride deflowre:
Gather the Rose of loue, whilest yet is time,
Whilst louing thou mayst loued be with equall crime.

Robert Herrick's "To the Virgins, to Make Much of Time" (1648) makes the same point, but with considerably less subtlety:

Gather ye rosebuds while ye may
    Old time is still a-flying;
And this same flower that smiles today
    Tomorrow will be dying.

ABOVE: *Seeming to float in air, these roses at Roseraie Bagatelle, Paris, encase rope swags to form glamorous yet effective fences.* OPPOSITE: *In Chipping Camden, this shower of yellow roses creates a magnificent garden out of the side of the house.*

THE GLORY OF ROSES

An interesting twist on the theme of ephemerality of youth and beauty occurs in the paired poems, Christopher Marlowe's "The Passionate Shepherd to his Love" (1599) and Sir Walter Raleigh's "The Nymph's Reply to the Shepherd" (1600). Marlowe's shepherd offers the invitation, "Come live with me and be my love. . . ."

> And I will make thee beds of roses
> And a thousand fragrant posies,
> A cap of flowers, and a kirtle
> Embroidered all with leaves of myrtle.

The passionate shepherd speaks as if youthful love lasts forever, but Raleigh's nymph reminds him otherwise.

> Thy gowns, thy shoes, thy beds of roses,
> Thy cap, thy kirtle, and thy posies
> Soon break, soon wither, soon forgotten—
> In folly ripe, in reason rotten.

Roses falling from the weathered stone walls add to the cachet of Scotney Castle, Kent, as one of England's most romantic planned landscapes.

THE GLORY OF ROSES

Poetry and folklore are closely related, and yet distinct. The poet has a name by which to be known, and it is generally the poetry that produces the kind of objective immortality that occurs when one's writings survive one's physical death. Folklore is by definition anonymous, the result of the collective shaping of traditions by many hands, over many generations. And the rose also has had its place in folklore, even if many of the meanings it has born have died with the disappearance, in most of the modern world, of the oral traditions of sayings and stories. Folklore today is more likely to be found in books in libraries than to be an active element within the human community. And the lore of the rose is often contradictory. A single example will suffice. In Scotland, as late as the middle of the nineteenth century, it was regarded as bad luck for a bride to carry a bridal bouquet with red roses in it. One possible interpretation of this superstition is that the bride would die young; roses do have their associations with death. (These associations go back to Adonis and to Christ, but they are

These fully extended rose blooms are graceful and beautiful, but the points of their petals bring to mind the thorns below.

much wider: in Switzerland, an old euphemism for graveyard is *Rosengarten*—"Rose garden.") But another Scottish legend held that it was good luck for the father of the bride to give her a bouquet of red roses to carry at the wedding.

Consistency of meaning is sometimes not to be found in these old folk beliefs, but they still have the power to fascinate. English lore held that if a woman picks three roses on Midsummer's Eve, buries one under a yew, another in a grave, and then sleeps with the third under her pillow, it will bring back a straying lover. Another piece of legendary advice held that all that was necessary to determine one's true lover was to name rose petals for each of one's suitors and put them in water: the one that stayed afloat the longest would tell the tale. In Bulgarian traditional lore, roses were more closely associated with witches than lovers. Sir James George Frazer

Such appropriateness of form and beauty leads one to imagine that roses have adorned this manor wall on the Isle of Wight for generations.

reported in *The Golden Bough* the Bulgarian custom of having cows walk over smoldering rose petals on Saint George's Day to protect them against witches. On the same day, branches of rosebushes would be put on barn doors to keep witches from using them as mounts to fly through the air.

In no folk tale does the rose figure as prominently as in the story of Sleeping Beauty. In this story, collected and given a final form by the brothers Grimm, a king and queen long for many years to have a child. When they have almost abandoned hope, they have a daughter, whose name in German means "Rose Briar." To celebrate her birth, they invite the kingdom's fairies to dine, but there are thirteen fairies (an unlucky number) and only twelve plates for guests, so one fairy is not invited. At the dinner, each guest makes a wish for the infant's future—a wish that will come true, because fairies have supernatural gifts. The twelfth fairy is about to offer her wish, when the thirteenth arrives. Angry at having been slighted, she horrifies everyone by uttering her wish that the child, at age fifteen, will prick her finger on a distaff and die. The twelfth fairy, however, still has her wish to make, and she wishes that instead of dying at fifteen, young Rose Briar will fall into a deep sleep for one hundred years.

The king and queen want to take no chances, so they collect every distaff in the kingdom. But on her fifteenth birthday, the princess discovers in their castle a secret doorway and a staircase leading to a tiny room, where she finds an old woman spinning. She touches the distaff of the spinning wheel, cutting her finger, and as the first drops of blood appear, she falls into a swoon. Her parents put her in a bed, and as she sleeps, the whole castle also falls asleep. The cook stops kneading her bread. The fire goes out in the hearth. The king and queen join their daughter in slumber.

All round the castle, briars begin to grow, enclosing it in their tight and thorny embrace. The story spreads that inside the thicket of roses

A medieval rhyme describes a rose's fringed sepals: In summer's day, in sultry weather/Five brethren were born together/Two had beards and two had none/And the other had half a one.

sleeps a beautiful young princess, who will awaken when a prince penetrates the briars and kisses her cheek. As the years pass, many princes make the effort to get past the roses and they all die in the attempt. But on the day that marks the hundredth anniversary of Rose Briar's pricking her finger, another prince appears. The roses around the castle have burst into full bloom for the very first time. They offer him no impediment, and he makes his way into the castle without a single scratch, a single tear in his garments. He kisses the princess. She wakes up. So do the king and the queen. The cook starts kneading her bread again. Flames spring up in the hearth. The prince and the princess get married, and everyone lives happily ever after.

The story is charming. My mother read it to me over and over when I was a child in Texas and it always fascinated me—even though there were no castles, no royalty, and no fairies in Texas. I read it in my turn to our own children. But by then I had read a lot of Sigmund Freud and a bit of

These sudden bursts of yellow are welcome sights which stir the heart for reasons which reason need not know.

THE GLORY OF ROSES

Carl Jung, enough to know that the story of Sleeping Beauty begged for a psychological interpretation. There were the numbers to ponder, first of all—twelve plates, the malevolent thirteenth fairy, the benevolent twelfth one and the merciful fact that she was the last to utter her wish and moderate the curse, the fifteenth birthday of the princess, and the hundred years she slumbered. The erotic meanings of the story are also almost embarrassingly plain. Fifteen marks the end of puberty, the awakening of sexuality. The thorny roses around the castle protect a virgin, echoing the roses in the enclosed gardens that protected the Virgin Mary. Their bursting into blossom, the welcome they at last grant to the prince who will awaken the sleeping princess with a kiss, symbolizes the arrival of sexual maturity and the forsaking of virginity guarded so long and so well. And the journey of the prince unscathed through the briars to find and claim his own Sleeping Beauty, his own Rose Briar, draws on the same deep well of psychosexual meaning as does *The Romance of the Rose*.

True to Candace Wheeler's words, one can see in the rose "an inner fascination, a subtle witchery, a hidden charm which it has and other flowers have not . . ."

THE GLORY OF ROSES

Roses have had their political meanings as well as their religious and amatory ones. England's War of the Roses (1453–85) may have had a pretty name, as names for wars go, but the conflict was a bitter one that brought the country near to anarchy. This civil war originated with the weak rule of Henry VI (1421–71), who became king during his infancy, so that his country was ruled for many years by a regent. Even after he became king in fact as well as name, he was unable to control the rival houses of York and Lancaster, which had as their respective emblems the white rose and the red. As Shakespeare told it in *Henry VI*, Richard Plantagenet, of the House of York, stood in the Temple Gardens challenging the other nobles present to choose the white rose and side with him; the Duke of Somerset, a Lancastrian, repeated the challenge with the red rose.

Here in the Roman Forum the fleeting magnificence of roses may serve as a reminder of how the mighty have fallen.

THE GLORY OF ROSES

Shakespeare's imagined version of the speeches delivered at this crucial turning in English history follows.

RICHARD PLANTAGENET:
    Let him that is a true-born gentleman
    And stands upon the honour of his birth,
    If he suppose that I have pleaded truth,
    From off this brier pluck a white rose with me.

SOMERSET:
    Let him that is no coward and no flatterer,
    But dare maintain the party of the truth,
    Pluck a red rose from off this thorn with me.

WARWICK:
    I love no colours; and without all colour
    Of base insinuating flattery
    I pluck this white rose with Plantagenet.

SUFFOLK:
    I pluck this red rose with young Somerset.

The result, Shakespeare wrote in commentary through Warwick's voice, is that—

    The brawl today
    Grown to this faction in the Temple Garden
    Shall send, between the red rose and the white,
    A thousand souls to death and deadly night.

In the ensuing conflict, sometimes one noble house was in control, sometimes the other. Edward of York took the throne in 1461 but then died, leaving two small sons. Their uncle imprisoned them in the Tower of London, in all likelihood was responsible for their murders, and assumed the throne as Richard III. After Richard's defeat and his death in battle in 1485, Henry VII became king and joined his own House of Lancaster with the House of York by marrying Elizabeth of York. The new dynasty had its own floral emblem, the Tudor rose, in which the outer petals of deep red surround the white petals at the center. The so-called York and Lancaster rose, in which magenta-red petals commingle somewhat confusedly with white ones, originated a century later, well after the

---

THE GLORY OF ROSES

wounds left in the English body politic by civil and dynastic warfare had been healed.

The rose has also been taken to symbolize nations and lesser political units. It is the official flower of Great Britain, Honduras, Iran, Romania, and Czechoslovakia, a fact which surely makes it one of the few items on which all these countries agree. In the United States, the rose has long been the state flower of Georgia, Iowa, and North Dakota, and I suppose I must say the district flower of Washington, D.C. In 1959 legislation was introduced in the U.S. Congress to make it the national flower, but no law was passed, probably because of the late Sen. Everett Dirksen's campaign (ill-advised I think) to plump for the marigold—and perhaps because some wiser souls favored the yucca, a quintessentially North American plant and a noble one. The rose, however, did become the official flower of the United States in 1986 when Congress unanimously passed legislation introduced by Rep. Lindy Boggs and Sen. Lloyd Bentsen. The whole

Even in decline, the petals of a pale ruby rose in sunlight can catch the onlooker's breath and prompt a philosophical sigh.

country thus joined rose cities like Pasadena, California, and Portland, Oregon in taking the flower as its emblem. Our recently adopted national flower is no particular rose, just a generic one.

In the Victorian culture of the nineteenth century in both America and Great Britain, the grander political and theological symbolism of the rose was swept away in a flood of sentimentality about personal relationships between men and women. There developed elaborate systems about a vocabulary or language of flowers. Giving another person a particular flower conveyed a particular message, sometimes altering if the flower were presented upside down, or if it were given with the left hand rather than the right. The association between a plant and its supposed meaning or message is difficult to fathom today. Why the pimpernel could mean either "change" or "assignation," why the pineapple expressed the sentiment "you are perfect," or why the pitch pine stood for "philosophy"— these stand as puzzles and conundrums. But books on the language of

In Christian lore red roses symbolize the blood of martyrs; in Roman legend they were the result of Cupid's spilled cup of wine.

THE GLORY OF ROSES

THE GLORY OF ROSES

flowers abounded in the nineteenth century, and they were often the bestsellers of their day.

A representative example of such works is Mrs. Sarah Josepha Hale's *Flora's Interpreter and Fortuna Flora*, published in Boston in 1856. According to Mrs. Hale, the burgundy rose meant "simplicity and beauty." A fresh white rose meant merely "sadness," but if it were withered it conveyed "despair." The yellow rose meant "let us forget." *Flora's Interpreter* goes on to give the messages of some thirty other kinds of roses, but it is well to note that two lovers sending each other floral messages were in urgent need of possessing the same codebook. Another book, Catherine H. Waterman's *Flora's Lexicon* published in Boston in 1858, states forthrightly that sending a lover a yellow rose was an accusation of infidelity—not necessarily to be excused with the words "let us forget."

But even as these books were multiplying (plagiarism was frequent) and enjoying huge popularity, the possibility that any particular rose could have a specific meaning was beginning to vanish. For one thing, since the early decades of the nineteenth century, hybridizers have brought new roses into being at an exponential rate, until their great numbers exhausted the range of messages lovers might exchange between themselves.

There was, however, a much greater reason for the collapse of the idea that there was a language of flowers, a system of meanings shared between the plant kingdom and the human race. From the time of the Greek gods and of the Middle Eastern vegetation demigods like Adonis or Dionysus, through the Middle Ages and even the Renaissance, it had been possible to believe that plants had meanings we could decipher and understand. The old medical Doctrine of Signatures of the medieval herbalists and physicians had held that God gave certain healing properties to certain plants and then marked them to indicate their uses. A plant with heart-shaped leaves was sure to be useful in treating coronary disease, and kidney-

An intricate stone fence, a black urn, a white fence post—all are given continuity by the overflowing generosity of this luscious rose display.

THE GLORY OF ROSES

shaped leaves indicated properties for dealing with kidney ailments. The human race stood at the center of all creation, able to discover within it intrinsic meanings and messages. We could take delight in roses, because roses were given for our delight or even for our religious edification.

We know better now. For one thing, plant symbolism is not the same in every culture. The Chinese, who grew roses in their gardens and who contributed in the early nineteenth century species of roses that bore genes that would utterly transform roses in Europe and America, found no meaning at all in them. In China, where chrysanthemums and peonies and even lespedezas, or bush clovers, have always been rich in symbolic meanings, the rose meant nothing, stood for nothing, had nothing to say at all. This cultural difference shows clearly that the meaning that we think we find in flowers, we ourselves have put there. Flowers may have uses, but they really have nothing to say at all.

In soft sunlight this floribunda rose has a purity and style evocative of its name, Ivory Fashion.

THE GLORY OF ROSES

In 1859, the year after *Flora's Lexicon* appeared, Charles Darwin's *Origin of Species* was published. It was the second of two mortal wounds received by humanity's attempts to anthropomorphize the world. The first blow, late in the eighteenth century, had been Linnaeus's classification of plants based on the understanding that in flowering plants the flowers were sexual organs, part of the ways in which plants contrived to reproduce themselves. A rose no longer merely symbolized sexuality, it was itself sexual.

As for Darwin's theory of evolution through natural selection, the English clergyman Canon Ellacombe fully understood its revolutionary impact on our thinking about plants. In his delightful book *In a Gloucestershire Garden* (1895), Ellacombe wrote:

> The old idea that plants were created in order that fruits and other products useful and pleasant to man might be brought into existence, and for

Climbing rambler roses at Roseraie Bagatelle in Paris are supported not only on conventional pergolas, but on rope swags draped from pillar to pillar.

these purposes only, has long been exploded, and we now believe that the whole life of a plant is directed to the one object of forming seed for the continuance of the life of the plant. Not for the sake of the beautiful flowers has the plant gone through its life: the beautiful flowers themselves were only one step onward in the formation of the seed.

It may be added that this gentle, flower-loving Victorian priest saw no conflict between Darwinism and Christianity, for he went on to write, "It may interest any who take up the subject to note how often in the New Testament the mysteries of the kingdom of heaven are compared to the mysteries of seed life, and how the Great Teacher Himself told us of man's ignorance on such a common everyday thing as the growth of a seed."

Flowers come into being and they pass out of being, but they have no meanings whatever where we are concerned. They play to another audi-

ABOVE: *Roses seem as critical to public gardens as public gardens are to civilization, and the common gardens in Tours, France, give testament to both.*
OPPOSITE: *These roses with lamb's ears at their base promise enchantment through the garden gate.*

THE GLORY OF ROSES

ence entirely. They mean something to bees and other insect pollinators. They mean something to themselves as being the partial instruments of the reproduction or continuance of their kind. With roses, as with indeed all other flowers, we are voyeurs in the full sense of this term. We look at roses with two eyes only, and thus we can have no idea of what they look like to a honeybee, with its more than twelve thousand lenses—in a set of five eyes, two compound and three simple—that are capable of perceiving the ultraviolet light that we cannot and incapable of perceiving the red light that we can. Similarly, the fragrance of roses and many other flowers may so please us that we gather them for nosegays, distill their essences into substances used in perfumes and in cooking, and associate them with our deepest and most powerful memories and desires; but again, we are olfactory onlookers—not in the main game at all.

Since Darwin's time and the rise of modern biological science we have never been able to look at roses in the old ways again. Roses are, intrin-

Even a rather forlorn climbing rose bestows the pleasures of a garden on a utilitarian spot.

sically, meaningless. But so are the notes of a musical scale. So are the ingredients that go into tempera or oil paint. So are the metaphors that enable us to compare two things to one another that are basically dissimilar. The human race may no longer be able to find meanings, but we have come to understand that we can create them. The notes of a musical scale can be so used and transformed as to become the B-Minor Mass. Paint can become Botticelli's *Birth of Venus*, with its blowing roses and its goddess of love arising from the sea. Metaphors may become the Vision of God—or intense sexual desire—captured in the image of a white rose unfolding or a red one still in bud.

And we, after long practice in making gardens, including gardens of roses, can now make roses, or at least bend our efforts and our will and our knowledge of plants to bring new roses into being.

Nothing seems as delicate in color, in texture, in form, as the petals of roses.

INDEX

BIBLIOGRAPHY

Austin, David. *The Heritage of the Rose.* Woodbridge, U.K.: The Antique Collectors' Club, 1988.

Breck, Joseph. *The Flower Garden.* New York: Sexton, 1851.

Brookes, John. *Gardens of Paradise: The History and Design of the Great Islamic Gardens.* New York: New Amsterdam Books, 1987.

Christopher, Thomas. *In Search of Lost Roses.* New York: Summit Books, 1989.

Culpeper, Nicholas. *Complete Herbal.* 1653. Reprint. Secaucus, N.J.: Chartwell Books, 1985.

Earle, Alice Morse. *Old Time Gardens.* New York: Macmillan, 1901.

————. *Sun-Dials and Roses of Yesterday.* New York: Macmillan, 1902.

Ellacombe, Canon. *In a Gloucestershire Garden.* London: Edward Arnold, 1895.

Fagan, Gwen. *Roses at the Cape of Good Hope.* Cape Town: Breestrat-Publikasies, 1988.

Fisher, John. *The Companion to Roses.* Topsfield, Mass. Salem House, 1987.

Gerard, John. *The Herball, or General History of Plants.* 2nd ed. 1633. Reprint. New York: Dover, 1975.

Gordon, Jean. *Pageant of the Rose.* Woodstock, Vt.: Red Rose Publications, 1961.

Hedrick, U.P. *A History of Horticulture in America.* Rev. ed., with an addendum by Elisabeth Woodburn. Portland, Ore.: Timber Press, 1988.

Hole, S. Reynolds. *A Book About Roses.* 11th ed. London: Edward Arnold, 1901.

Jekyll, Gertrude. *The Gardener's Essential Gertrude Jekyll.* Boston: Godine, 1986.

Krüssman, Gerd. *The Complete Book of Roses.* Translated by Gerd Krussman and Nigel Raban. Portland, Ore.: Timber Press, 1981.

Lawrence, Elizabeth. *Gardening for Love: The Market Bulletins.* Durham, N.C.: Duke University Press, 1987.

Le Rougetel, Hazel. *A Heritage of Roses.* Owings Mills, M.D.: Stemmer House, 1988.

Parkinson, John. *Paradisi in Sole: Paradisus Terrestris.* 1629. Facsimile ed. London: Methuen, 1904.

Parsons, Samuel B. *The Rose: Its History, Poetry, Culture, and Classification.* New York: Wiley & Putnam, 1847.

Paterson, Allen. *The History of the Rose.* London: William Collins, 1983.

Paul, William. *The Rose Garden.* London: Sherwood, Gilbert, & Piper, 1848.

Robinson, William. *The English Flower Garden.* 15th ed. 1934. Reprint. New York: The Amaryllis Press, 1984.

Shepherd, Roy E. *History of the Rose.* New York: Macmillan, 1954.

Thacker, Christopher. *The History of Gardens.* Berkeley and Los Angeles: University of California Press, 1979.

Thaxter, Celia. *An Island Garden.* Boston: Houghton Mifflin, 1894.

Wheeler, Candace. *Content in a Garden.* Boston: Houghton Mifflin, 1902.

Wilder, Louise Beebe. *The Fragrant Path.* New York: Macmillan, 1932.

Designed by
Mary Vetek Inabnit
Diana M. Jones
Composed in Janson and Bembo
by Trufont Typographers, Inc.,
Hicksville, New York
Printed and bound by
Toppan Printing Company, Ltd.,
Tokyo, Japan